MISSION POSSIBLE:
REACHING THE NEXT GENERATION
THROUGH THE SMALL CHURCH

DR. TERRY W. DORSETT

CROSSBOOKS
PUBLISHING

CrossBooks™
A Division of LifeWay
1663 Liberty Drive
Bloomington, IN 47403
www.crossbooks.com
Phone: 1-866-879-0502

First published by CrossBooks 02/27/2012

ISBN: 978-1-4627-1379-0 (sc)
ISBN: 978-1-4627-1383-7 (hc)
ISBN: 978-1-4627-1378-3 (e)

Library of Congress Control Number: 2012901333

Printed in the United States of America

This book is printed on acid-free paper.

Previous Works by Dr. Terry W. Dorsett

Developing Leadership Teams in the Bivocational Church
July 2010 by CrossBooks Publishing

Bible Brain Teasers: Fun Adventures through the Bible
July 2011 by Lulu Press

Creating Effective Partnerships—
Strategies for Increasing Kingdom Impact
December 2011 by Lulu Press

With deep appreciation to all the young adults in my life who have helped me see the world through new eyes, especially my own three children, Katie, Taylor, and Jonas.

CONTENTS

FOREWORD

Though many small churches are struggling to reach their changing communities, other small churches are doing an amazing job of impacting people for Christ in spite of limited resources and manpower. We are finally beginning to see a change in how leaders of mission organizations, denominations, and training schools perceive the small church. Books, magazine articles, and online voices are appearing that acknowledge the value healthy small churches have in America. After decades of fascination with large churches and sprawling mega-campuses, especially in suburbs of metropolitan areas, some leaders are brave enough to ask: Is it only bigger churches that can lead the way in kingdom expansion, or can small churches do so as well? Is bigger always better?

My friend Terry Dorsett is one of the few to wave the flag for small churches, believing they have something to teach the broader kingdom of God about how church can be done effectively. After I met Terry online in 2010, we began to exchange ideas and articles that focused on our mutual interest in helping smaller churches, and the pastors who serve them, to be healthier. Now seldom a week that goes by when we do not touch base with each other. I consider him a friend and kindred spirit. I am so grateful for the enthusiastic encouragement and resources Terry brings to pastors of smaller churches.

Smaller churches often focus on what they cannot do rather than on what they can do. They tend to focus on their perceived weaknesses rather than on their obvious strengths. This creates a self-defeating cycle where small churches tend to say, "If we were just a little larger, we could do so much more." Through his blog (www. terrydorsett.com), as well as his books, Terry seeks to help smaller churches overcome this tendency.

In Terry's first book, *Developing Leadership Teams in the Bivocational Church*, readers learned that smaller churches can be healthy and thrive even without a fully funded pastor by mastering the art of delegation. Now, with the book you are holding in your hands, Terry demonstrates how the small church, especially those in small towns and rural areas, can be effective in winning the next generation for Christ.

It has been my experience, both as a pastor for thirty years and now as a consultant and coach specializing in smaller congregations, that there is nothing a larger church can do that a smaller church is unable to do. Actually, some studies claim a smaller church does many things better than their larger friends. But it is not whether the smaller church or the larger church is better. What is important is that every church, regardless of size, fulfills the call God has for them in the community where God has placed them. This book, though focused on smaller churches in small towns and rural areas, actually offers principles and ideas that will be helpful to any size of church in any area. Those who are leaders in smaller churches will find this book brimming with helpful ideas. Those who are leaders in larger churches will find this book equally helpful. God has given each church everything it needs to do the things He has called those churches to do. Everything! We just need to get busy doing it.

As you read *Mission Possible: Reaching the Next Generation through the Small Church*, do so carefully and prayerfully. The Holy Spirit is about to share with you hope and strategies that will help your church, regardless of size, have a dynamic impact upon the next generation.

Dave Jacobs,
Founder of Small Church Pastor, Inc.

CHAPTER ONE

GRANDPA'S CHURCH IS STRUGGLING

Mrs. Smith rose early on Sunday morning to bake homemade cinnamon rolls for her family, while her husband walked the family dog, Fido, down their tree-lined suburban street. When Mr. Smith returned home with the dog, he was very excited. "Sally and Tom from across the street are going to church with us this morning," he exclaimed to Mrs. Smith.

Mrs. Smith's heart overflowed with joy as she made her way upstairs to wake her son and daughter so they would have time for breakfast before going to Sunday school.

About an hour later, as the Smith family drove down the street in their minivan, they saw Sally and Tom pull out of their driveway and follow them the two miles downtown to First Church on Main Street. Mrs. Smith thought to herself, *What a wonderful way to spend a Sunday morning!*

Such idyllic scenes may have been common across America in the past, but in our increasingly post-Christian society, such situations are acted out less often. In this current era, it is much more likely that Mr. Smith and Ms. Jones will live together for years, raising their kids together without feeling the need to be married. The neighbors across

> The neighbors across the street could well be a married couple named Tom and John.

1

the street could be a married couple named Tom and John. The two couples are more likely to go camping together for the weekend than to attend church, and if they do happen to attend church, it is probably for a special service at either Christmas or Easter.

By all accounts, the North American church is enduring difficult times. Most Christians realize that churches are struggling to reach out to the surrounding community, but people are not sure why churches are struggling or what they, as individuals, can do about it. Though there are many reasons churches are struggling, the primary reason is that North American culture is experiencing rapid change, while most churches remain unchanged. Therefore, churches are struggling to reach the generations that are emerging from this new culture.

Some churches have made it clear that they do not intend to change, even if it means their membership will keep shrinking. These churches have ignored culture and vainly hope that people will come to faith even though—because of cultural differences—those people cannot understand the church's message. Other churches have adjusted their core values and tossed out all their time-honored traditions in the hope that the community will respond positively to their radical change. Such churches have lost much of their identity and are frequently still in decline as they abandon biblical principles and find themselves adrift in an ocean of rapidly changing theology. Many evangelical churches are looking for a third option. These churches are willing to adopt certain levels of change to reach their community but are determined not to give up their core values and biblical principles in the process.

All three types of churches are struggling with changing culture and its impact on their congregations, but this book has been written specifically for the third type of churches, those that see the need for change but do not want to lose their core values and biblical principles in the process. Though American culture is always changing, the timeless truth of the gospel remains the same. How we communicate the gospel may change, but the gospel itself never changes. The gospel is relevant to all cultures in all time periods. We must hold true to the gospel while discovering new ways to communicate with a non-Christian culture.

Many experts have written effectively about how cities and urban areas are changing.[1] A number of fine books and well-written articles detail how urban churches have addressed cultural change.[2] Numerous urban churches and mega-churches have developed new ministry models to reach their communities. Large churches are building Starbucks coffee shops in their lobbies and health club—quality family life centers on their growing campuses. Some churches now use their spacious lobbies as art galleries. Others have professional-quality light and laser shows in their sanctuaries. Many large churches employ a variety of staff members to lead a growing number of programs aimed at reaching the next generation.

Many of these large, urban churches are successfully reaching the constantly evolving culture and the younger generations that have emerged from it. However, most of the ministry models used by large, urban churches do not fit the context of smaller churches, nor are they feasible in more rural areas or small towns. Few resources are being developed to help small churches and churches in rural areas impact their changing communities. This book is one effort to provide a practical resource to help small churches reach emerging generations in a biblical and culturally contextual way.

Though some small churches may question the validity of innovative outreach methods used by larger and more urban churches, this book does not seek to justify or attack such efforts. This book assumes that large, urban churches are led by godly, Spirit-filled individuals who have prayed through their decisions to use various innovative methods to reach the next generation. However, it is clear that while these methods may be appropriate in the right context, the majority of churches in North America are too small to do those things effectively.

In addition, whether small churches support or oppose such innovative methods is a moot point because they have neither the financial nor the personnel resources to implement these innovative methods. Regardless of available resources, small churches must not abandon the next generation to a life of spiritual and emotional pain without the hope that faith in Jesus Christ brings. Small churches must not abandon the next generation to an eternity in hell because the church cannot afford a Starbucks in the lobby or a laser light machine in the sanctuary. Small churches must find a way to reach the emerging generations. Small churches will have to learn new approaches without discarding their core values or theological distinctives.

Throughout this book, the terms "next generation," "young people," and "postmodern people" will be used interchangeably. This is technically inaccurate because not all postmodern people are young and not all young people in the next generation are postmodern.

> **Small churches must not abandon the next generation to an eternity in hell because they cannot afford a Starbucks in the lobby or a laser light machine in their sanctuary.**

However, the majority are; therefore, it is appropriate to use these terms interchangeably in the context of this discussion.

Some church leaders might be unclear on the definition of postmodernism. The term was first used in the 1870s but was not widely used until the late twentieth century and early twenty-first century. The term itself is primarily used by people with a modern worldview who are trying to understand the thinking processes of those with a postmodern worldview. People who hold to postmodernism themselves do not like to be classified, and therefore it is unlikely they will use the term to refer to themselves. Although whole books have been written to explain the term, I will give only a general explanation here to make the principles in this book easier to understand.

Postmodernism is the idea that individuals have both the intelligence and the right to decide for themselves what truth is. In the past, truth was a clearly defined fact that was generally accepted by each generation. Postmodern individuals see the definition of truth as less clear. As postmodern people search for truth, they base their conclusions on their own research, individual experiences, and personal relationships instead of on the truth accepted by their parents, government, or church. This does not mean postmodernists do not believe in truth; it just means they define truth for themselves. Postmodern people are quite comfortable with the concept that different people will come to different conclusions about the same subject and all of them have discovered the truth, even if such truths contradict each other. For most postmodern people, the concept of absolute truth does not exist. It has been replaced with a more personalized sense of truth that may vary from person to person.

It can be difficult to describe how postmodern people think because they do not like to be categorized. However, careful observation of their behaviors, combined with listening to what young people say and write, offer a glimpse of postmodernists' common characteristics. Dr. Earl Creps is the director of the doctor of ministry program at Assemblies of God Theological Seminary in Springfield, Missouri. He writes extensively on postmodernism. He has discovered:

> The average person influenced by postmodernism may never have heard a lecture or read a book about it. Nonetheless, the traits that embody the philosophy are all around us: the centrality of community, the primacy of experience, the subjectivity of truth, the complexity of human perception, the fragility of progress, the unreality of absolutes, the enormity of the spiritual [and] the plurality of worldviews.[3]

Other writers have compiled similar lists of postmodern traits that frequently appear in the next generation. If churches wish to effectively engage postmodern people with the gospel, they will have to deal with these common traits.

Postmodern people can be any age, but typically, the younger people are, the more likely they are to have a postmodern worldview. Dr. Jan W. van Deth, a political science professor at the University of Mannheim, and Elinor Scarbrough, a senior lecturer in government at the University of Essex and co-director of the Essex Summer School in Data Analysis and Collection, have studied postmodernism extensively. They have presented a number of papers and edited a book on the subject. Based on their studies, they conclude that "postmodern orientations are most common among young people and the well educated."[4]

There is no set age at which individuals suddenly decide to become postmodern. Instead, postmodern tendencies are more like a graph in which the younger a person is, the more postmodern his or her worldview is likely to be. This connection between age and postmodernism comes from a past when people had access to a limited amount of information, so it was harder for them to question truth. Because of this, older generations often believed what they were told because they did not have access to information that would lead them to think otherwise.

With the advent of technology, younger generations have become used to collecting information from a wide variety of sources, as have more-educated people. Even though much of the information collected may be inaccurate, it still makes younger generations question the validity of what others have told them. Instead, they want to discover truth for themselves. This desire to discover one's own truth is the essence of postmodernism.

Contrary to what many Christians think, people with a postmodern worldview often consider themselves to be quite spiritual. However, they tend to pick and choose the pieces of spirituality they like from a variety of sources. They will not accept the church's traditional brand of spirituality without personal exploration, experiences, and relationships. Since so many traditional evangelical churches expect blanket acceptance, postmodern young people have struggled to remain involved in traditional evangelical churches in recent years.

For several years I have known Li-Jin,[5] who is an exceptionally bright student at one of the finest colleges in New England. One of Li-Jin's parents is a Christian; the other is a Buddhist. Li-Jin often refers to himself as a Christian Buddhist. After I had extensive conversations with Li-Jin, it was clear he had spent a considerable amount of time reading books by both Christian and Buddhist authors and melded certain aspects of each religion into his own personal belief system. Though parts of each religion clearly contradict the other and the two worldviews are incompatible as an integrated faith system, in Li-Jin's mind, this melded religion makes sense. Li-Jin essentially created his own religion—his personal brand of spiritual truth. Not only did he get to pick the parts of each religion that he liked best, but he was also able to avoid disappointing either of his parents. This eclectic kind of spirituality, in which pieces of different religions are combined into a new belief system, is becoming quite common among members of the next generation. As one can imagine, small churches will have to work harder to reach people like Li-Jin. But they can be reached!

After reading some of the more-popular books on postmodern evangelism and church growth, leaders of small churches may be under the false impression they must toss out everything they practice and believe in to find some radical new way of doing church before they can reach someone like Li-Jin.[6] While many churches may indeed need to examine some of their methods and programs, they do not need to throw out everything and start over. Some simple adjustments in three areas will allow small churches to reach out to the next generation: helping the church regain its position as the social center of the community; helping the church regain its position as the ceremonial center of the community; and using the church's facilities as an outreach tool.

Though these three areas have been historically strong in most churches, they have begun to slip in effectiveness as the culture has become more secular. Church leaders need to consider any changes that might help them reverse the decline churches have experienced in these three areas. The first five chapters of this book will address these three areas. Some call the concepts in the first half of this book "attractional evangelism." If that term is unfamiliar, do not worry—it will be explained later.

The last six chapters of the book will cover a fourth area of where change is needed. Those chapters will address philosophical changes churches might want to consider to engage the next generation. These philosophical changes have a number of practical applications that will also be discussed. This area will require a greater degree of change for churches and will therefore entail greater struggle. Some people refer to the concepts in the second half of this book as "missional evangelism." That term will be explained later as well. These philosophical concepts have purposely been addressed last so church leaders can work their way up to them. Some churches may choose not to implement the ideas from the second half of the book. Though that may result in reaching fewer postmodern people, if the church implements at least some of the ideas of the first half of the book, they will be reaching some postmodern people. Reaching some is better than reaching none, and sometimes churches can endure only so much change at one time.

Read the entire book with a heart that is seeking to hear from the Lord. Then prayerfully implement some of the ideas from the first half of the book. As the Lord leads, consider how the ideas from the second half of the book might be implemented as well. Keep in mind that the goal is to bring glory to God by sharing the Christian faith with the changing community around our churches without abandoning biblical principles in the process. It can be a fine line. It will take discernment, prayer, and a deep reliance on the leading of the Holy Spirit, but it can be done.

The terms attractional evangelism and missional evangelism might be unfamiliar to some readers. Though the two types of evangelism overlap in some ways, in general attractional evangelism is an effort to attract people to the church and its programs, events, and ministries. Once people show up, the church makes an effort to evangelize them. In contrast, missional evangelism is primarily an effort to go outside the four walls of the facility and be on a mission to do evangelism in the community. Missional churches focusing on that style of evangelism are often involved in service projects in the community or in civic organizations as a way to connect with and evangelize non-Christians.

Attractional evangelism is often event or program driven, whereas missional evangelism is often lifestyle or relationship driven. Though some evangelism experts tend to promote one way as being better than the other, in reality, it should not be either/or; it should be both/and. Moving beyond the walls of the church through missional involvement in the community is very important. However, since the very nature of the church is to gather people together for worship, prayer, fellowship, and teaching, at some point the previously unchurched have to be gathered for the church to be considered effective. Whether that gathering is held in a house, a Gothic cathedral, a small family chapel, or a mega-church campus, the principle of Hebrews 10:25 remains the same: "Let us not give up meeting together, as some are in the habit of doing, but let us encourage one another—and all the more as you see the Day approaching" (NIV).

The Mass Evangelism Team at the North American Mission Board of the Southern Baptist Convention recently compiled results on the effectiveness of both missional and attractional evangelism. Jerry Pipes, leader of that team, has said:

> A lot of churches have pursued a missional approach to evangelism and church growth to the neglect of attractional evangelistic events that will draw people in. That is like asking a pilot flying over the Pacific Ocean whether he wants his right wing or his left wing. The answer is you need both wings—both missional methodologies and an attractional model.[7]

Small churches should desire to use both missional and attractional evangelism to reach their communities for Christ. These two philosophical views on evangelism are not contradictory to each other. This book seeks to show small churches how they can blend the two types of evangelism to effectively reach their changing communities.

Chapter Two

What Happened to Grandpa's Town?

In the stereotypical small American community, everyone knows everyone, and people have many interpersonal connections through school, church, and community organizations. In those communities, it is common for many people to be related by blood or marriage to a significant portion of the local population. All the natives know the unofficial way of how things get done, which usually has a lot more to do with who a person knows than official policies and procedures. Small communities are often more conservative than urban areas. Small communities are normally more respectful of religion in general, though not everyone in the community will go to church. Such communities are often more Caucasian than urban areas, report lower crime rates, and frequently have a lower educational level than the national average. While many aspects of that stereotype were probably accurate in the past, small American communities are experiencing rapid change today. Though the old stereotypes of small towns and rural areas can still be found, they are increasingly the minority culture in many areas.

It is important to note that such stereotypes make broad statements about entire population groups or communities and may not be true of each individual within that population group or community. However, such stereotypes can be helpful to paint a big picture of the similarities in a community. It is important to note that postmodernism has various sub-groups that will not fit the general stereotype. It is also important to note that individuals have unique personal characteristics that may defy such narrow classifications. However, in the interest of setting the stage for what many churches are dealing with in their communities, it will be helpful to use some broadly generalized statements.

As well-educated and socially active families have grown frustrated with urban life and disenchanted with suburban sprawl, many are moving to small towns and rural areas. These newcomers often have a postmodern worldview. Sometimes people who grew up in a small town or rural area and later moved to a city will move back to their hometowns and bring with them newly acquired postmodern ideas. But more often, postmodern people who move to a less-populated area are urbanites seeking to escape all the problems of urban living. With the advent of computer and Internet technology, urbanites can now live anywhere and retain the same income level that previously could be found only in the city.

But it is not only newcomers who are changing the nature of small communities. The same technology that made it possible for outsiders to move in has also brought the outside world to small towns and rural communities. Teenagers from small towns and rural areas can now be just as connected and up-to-date on music, clothing styles, and philosophical concepts as their urban counterparts. Adults from rural and small towns are now exposed to more progressive ideas and concepts than ever before, and some of them are buying into these new ideas.

This rapid change in the nature of small-town America has had a significant impact on local churches. In the past three years, a number of articles have been published about the decline of Christianity in America. CNN published the results of a March 9, 2009, poll that concluded, "America is a less Christian nation than it was 20 years ago."[1] The

> **Teenagers from small towns and rural areas can now be just as connected and up-to-date on music, clothing styles and philosophical concepts as their urban counterparts.**

article went on to explain, "Seventy-five percent of Americans call themselves Christian, according to the American Religious Identification Survey from Trinity College in Hartford, Connecticut. In 1990, the figure was 86 percent."[2] That is a drop of more than 10 percent in only twenty years.

After studying the influence of Christianity in American society, Jon Meacham, the editor of *Newsweek* magazine, concluded, "While we remain a nation decisively shaped by religious faith, our politics and our culture are, in the main, less influenced by movements and arguments of an explicitly Christian character than they were even five years ago."[3] If such a trend continues unchecked, the organized church will remain in serious trouble.

Ken Ham, founder and president of Answers in Genesis, an organization that promotes a biblical view of creation, is concerned about how few young adults there are in many of the churches where he speaks. He enlisted America's Research Group to study why young people were leaving the church. Based on the results of the study, Ham wrote a book entitled *Already Gone*. The results of the survey are shocking: "95 percent of 20 to 29-year-old evangelicals attended church regularly during their elementary and middle school years. Only 55 percent went to church during high school. And by college, only 11 percent were still attending church."[4] Ham concluded, "The next generation of believers is draining from the churches, and it causes me great personal and professional concern."[5]

Ed Stetzer, president of Lifeway Research, has written extensively about this issue as well. Referring to the decreasing number of young believers, Stetzer says, "This is sobering news that the church needs to change the way it does ministry."[6] There is no arguing that the statistics reveal that fewer young adults identify with the Christian religion now than ever before.

Though the numbers reveal a decline of Christianity at the national level, this does not mean that every church in every small town or rural area is facing imminent closure. A number of bright spots on the horizon demonstrate that small churches can grow in the current spiritual climate. Some of the most-encouraging examples are found in the most unlikely places. Vermont is a great example of a place where the next generation is being reached despite all the statistics that make it seem improbable.

The Green Mountain Baptist Association is an evangelical mission organization ministering in Vermont and affiliated with the Southern Baptist Convention. Founded in 1982, the association is dedicated to strengthening existing evangelical churches in Vermont and starting new Baptist churches in towns that are underserved spiritually. According to a December 2009 survey published in *USA Today*, Vermont is the least-religious state in America, with the lowest rate of church attendance in the nation.[7] Despite these less-than-stellar religious statistics, from 2001 to 2010, the Green Mountain Baptist Association grew from seventeen churches to thirty-seven churches, and attendance at Sunday morning worship services grew from just under nine hundred to over two thousand. Though statistically Vermont's Christian community is in decline, the Green Mountain Baptist Association is rapidly growing.

Other evangelical groups in Vermont are also experiencing significant growth. The Essex Alliance Church, which is affiliated with the Christian and Missionary Alliance, has skyrocketed in attendance. Fifteen years ago, it had a modest congregation of less than two hundred. In 2010 it is the largest church in the state of Vermont, with over one thousand who attend worship on a typical Sunday. Jeffrey McDonald, a reporter for the *Christian Science Monitor*, observed, "As liberal congregations die in a secularizing region, conservative churches with roots outside New England are replacing them with a passionate brand of faith that emphasizes saving souls-even in a land where many think there's nothing to be saved from."[8] This anomaly between the official statistics about Christianity in Vermont and the actual experience of evangelicals who minister in the state is proof that while some churches in small towns may be struggling, other churches in those same small towns are growing. This shows that changing communities can be reached.

Some disagreement exists about why Vermont is statistically the least-churched state in America yet still has such rapid growth in its evangelical community. The prevailing view of many evangelical Christian leaders in Vermont is that a large number of people who have called themselves Christians in the past did so out of tradition or habit, but many of those people never truly had a personal commitment to following Christ in their daily lives. This does not mean they were atheists; it just means that their Christianity was more a vague concept or in some cases was more akin to membership in a social club than having a deep personal faith in God. While such a commitment to Christianity has some social merit, it has significant spiritual weaknesses. The primary weakness with this less personal form of Christianity is that when it is tested, it will almost always collapse.

Cleary, a disconnect exists between the official statistics and the spiritual reality in Vermont. If this is true in Vermont, it also may be true across the rest of the nation. If this theory is accurate, real Christianity may not be in as much trouble as cultural Christianity. This is especially true among those in the twenty-something age bracket. Ed Stetzer's research discovered, "The percentage of 20-somethings attending weekly worship services has been rising since 2000, after a serious dip in the mid-1990s."[9] Stetzer went on to confirm, "The 2008 data showed another uptick, bringing attendance among evangelical 20-somethings back to what it was in 1972. Among non-evangelicals there was indeed a decline."[10]

Young adults are abandoning non-evangelical churches and being drawn to evangelical ones. Stetzer concludes, "Listening to some commentators, you might conclude that young adults had left the church. But that is not what the data tells us."[11] Many young adults who were not completely committed to the Christian faith have stopped identifying themselves as Christians. At the same time, a smaller number of young adults have become more committed to their faith, but they are expressing it through involvement in churches that are more evangelical in theology. This results in a statistical decline overall but a much more passionate faith for those who remain.

Young adults with only a nominal connection to Christianity have watched as the concept of Christianity has been severely tested in recent years. Too many Protestant television evangelists have gone bad, and too many Catholic priests have molested children. People who have only a vague Christian commitment have distanced themselves from the church under these circumstances. Therefore, the total number of people who indicate they are Christians has naturally dropped as individuals who were on the fringe no longer identify themselves as Christians. The result is a statistical oddity where fewer people think of themselves as Christians, though certain types of churches are rapidly growing. As the culture has changed, the less-robust form of Christianity has imploded. On the other hand, true Christianity, which focuses on a personal relationship with Jesus Christ rather than on manmade traditions, is thriving.

Small churches need to discover what makes some churches grow even though the culture is less Christian than before. Even though there are bright spots of spiritual renewal on the horizon and the decline in Christianity may not be quite as sharp as statistics say, few Christian

> **Small churches need to discover what it is that makes some churches grow even though the culture is less Christian than before.**

leaders in America would say that Christianity overall is growing. Something is obviously wrong with many churches. The problems lie mostly in the inability of the churches to connect with and retain the next generation. Postmodern young adults with only a nominal faith have wandered away from Christianity, and if the church does not do something about it, those young people probably will not come back.

CHAPTER THREE

THE SMALL CHURCH AS THE SOCIAL CENTER OF THE COMMUNITY

The smaller the community, the more likely it is that the church in that community was once its social center. This is a good historical reputation for a church to hold. Unfortunately, as communities have changed, many churches have lost that important role. However, postmodern people who move to a small community are often looking for social connections. Therefore, churches that seek to regain this role will find the next generation to be receptive.

Because social events are often limited in small communities, even people who have lived their entire lives in such communities often look for something interesting to do that engages them with others who have similar interests. Small churches should look for a variety of ways to enhance the concept of the church as the social center of the community to attract both long-term and new residents. Both of these groups are prime candidates for the church to reach, even if they have a different worldview than the church.

Washington Baptist Church is located in the middle of Washington, Vermont, a village of five hundred people. At one time, the church was the social center of the community, but in 1993, the church had dwindled to less than twenty active members and was facing possible closure. The church's denominational leadership encouraged the church to call a young pastor who would focus on reaching the next generation. They did so, and he led the church to host a variety of concerts, outdoor barbecues, and sports activities designed to help the church regain its position as the place where exciting social events happened.

The community responded positively to those efforts because in the collective consciousness of the community, the church had a long history of doing such events even though the church had not done them recently. When that young pastor moved to a new church in 2001, the church had returned to a place of health. The congregation had more than tripled in size and become significantly younger than it had been in many years. The congregation continued to host a variety of community events each year, and in 2007, the church called a second staff member to serve as a youth pastor to more effectively reach the next generation. In 2011 the church continued to be healthy and clearly remains the social center of the village.

The process of becoming the social center of a community includes establishing and maintaining connections with residents. Unfortunately, many small churches often never connect with postmodern people because they do not know how. Younger people are typically very technologically oriented. This means they socialize and communicate more via electronic media than in person. To reach these people, small churches must discover how to use Facebook, Twitter, text messaging, websites, and other technological opportunities to build relationships and promote events. These types of technological gateways are often the front door that the next generation comes through to discover the small church.

Postmodern people no longer look in the phone book for information. They search the Internet. If small churches do not have a website, they do not exist in the minds of most young people. Consequently, having a church website is no longer optional; it is a necessity. Starting a Facebook page for the church's youth group or any other ministry is also important for the same reason. A church might consider collecting everyone's cell phone number to send out text message announcements about church events. It is important for churches to embrace technology in every way possible. Though older generations tend to resist the use of technology as a means of communication because it seems impersonal, this is often the easiest and most effective way to connect with the younger generation. They do not view it as cold and impersonal at all. To them it is a natural form of communication.

Small churches may continue to do many of the same activities and programs that they have always done, but it is important for them to promote those programs and activities through twenty-first-century technological methods. It is the way people with a postmodern worldview gather information and make decisions about what to put on their social calendar.

Inviting people to church events is a classic form of attractional evangelism. Using technology to reach out into the community in a way that is culturally relevant is a more missional approach to evangelism. This is one example of how attractional and missional approaches can be combined to reach a more postmodern audience.

However, just having a nice website or an active Facebook page is not enough to help the church regain its position as the social center of the community. Remember, the church is really the people, not the building. Therefore, small churches should be looking for ways to engage people relationally to share the gospel with them.

It is difficult to engage people relationally until we have spent time with them. Relationship building is not a program. It is a process that requires face-to-face interaction. Technology can connect us to the next generation initially, but then we must use those connections to build real relationships.

For example, every Wednesday is Youth Night at Faith Community Church of Barre, Vermont, which is a blue-collar community of only 8,837. Though church attendance is affected by the various sports seasons, normally fifty-five to sixty-five teenagers participate each week. When the official program is over and the crowd begins to disperse, a few stragglers who do not yet want to go home linger behind. These stragglers enjoy being together. These teenagers often ask the deepest questions of the youth workers after most of the other youth have left. The leaders frequently end up at McDonald's with these stragglers for a late-night snack. The group sits around McDonald's laughing, talking, and eating, holding what they jokingly refer to as "McChurch."

Though casual observers watching the group at McDonald's may not realize what they are seeing, those who watch more closely will realize that it is very much a spiritual experience at the McChurch. In that moment, the group is being the church. Though they may not have their Bibles open in a formal Bible study, their lives are open, and they display the truths of the Bible lived out in real-life experience. Though they may not verbally sing praise songs to Jesus, their hearts are filled with praise, and the laughter on their lips honors the one for whom they live their lives. Though it might not look spiritual, what happens at McDonald's has a profound spiritual impact on those who regularly participate because they know they belong to a solid group of Christians who love God and one another.

A sense of belonging comes from the relationships that are built during this time at McDonald's. The relationships that are built there are as vital in the evangelism and discipleship process as the lesson that was taught during the regular church service. In a day when half of all marriages end in divorce and many children grow up isolated from their extended families, young people often do not have the support they need to live successful lives. Giving them safe, healthy, and wholesome places to be together builds a sense of community. When done in a Christian context, it can be one of the most effective tools the church can use to reach young people. Whether that sense of community is created in the actual church building or in a McDonald's, the result is the same. Young people need to feel like they belong. Because a sense of belonging is so important in this postmodern age, churches that fail to create that atmosphere will most likely fail to reach the next generation.

A significant contrast is growing between churches that have only a formal ministry aimed at reaching the next generation and those that are focused on building relationships with the next generation. Churches trying to reach young people in any fashion are to be commended, but churches with only a formal program will not reach as many young people for Christ as those that are focused on building relationships. Though social interaction is important to postmodern people of any age, it is absolutely essential to those under age thirty-five.

Len Hjalmarson, a Canadian pastor, author, and church consultant, writes regularly about how to reach postmodern young people. Hjalmarson concludes that postmodern people "reject authority of position in favor of authority in relationship."[1] Young people do not care who is in charge; they care about the person with whom they have a relationship. Basically, the relationship means everything to young people. Hjalmarson goes on to say:

> When church leaders fail to engage the postmodern [relationally], they risk becoming isolated from the culture they live in. This in turn guarantees that the church communities they build will gradually stagnate and die, becoming museum communities instead of missional communities.[2]

Likewise, when the church regains its position as the social center of the community by focusing on building relationships, it will begin to attract postmodern people under age thirty-five.

For those who struggle to understand the difference between building relationships and simply having a program, here are some thoughts to consider. A program is something that a church sponsors once or twice a week. It begins and ends at a specific time and is very structured in the way it functions. Such programs often have a core group, mostly consisting of people who have a long history of connection to the church. The program's participants

> Young people do not care who is in charge; they care about the person with whom they have a relationship.

seldom bring their friends to take part in the program. Many older adults in the church often see programs aimed at reaching the next generation as a drain on the budget, but they invest the money anyway because it seems like the right thing to do. Unfortunately, such programs are not very effective in the long term. Audrey Barrick, a writer for *The Christian Post*, frequently reports on trends impacting the church. In a 2007 article, Barrick reported that nearly two-thirds of teens who participate in youth programs will drop out of church during their college years.[3] Clearly, using a programs approach is not the most effective way to reach the next generation.

A relationship-based ministry, on the other hand, is quite different from a program-based effort. While a relationship-based ministry will include some structured programs, it also includes a lot of impromptu events. The people involved in these ministries spend a lot of time together. This time might be spent over a hamburger at McDonald's, ice cream at the local ice cream shop, or playing cards or games on a Wii. The people in this kind of ministry know each other, encourage each other, and are involved in one another's lives. Young adults who are part of such a ministry often come from outside the church and may take part in the church without any support from their families. The leaders of such ministries look for ways to include these young people in the overall life of the church because they enjoy being together. Older people in the church may see these young adults as a little unruly, but because they are excited about changed lives, they are usually committed to helping those young people despite the occasional frustrations members of the next generation bring to the church.

Relationship-based ministry takes more time, but it is the most effective way to reach those under thirty-five. Ed Stetzer says, "Programs must be the tool, not the goal."[4] Stetzer goes on to say, "Programming must give way to intentional relationships and community."[5] Programs have their place, but programs alone will not be sufficient to hold the interest of the next generation or help the church regain its position as the social center of the community.

Small churches may more readily regain their position as the social center of the community by using technology to connect with postmodernists. Such churches can then build relationships with those with whom they make connections. Those relationships will result in postmodernists showing interest once again in the church. Consequently, the church will then be able to more readily fulfill its mission of evangelism and discipleship.

CHAPTER FOUR

THE SMALL CHURCH AS THE CEREMONIAL CENTER OF THE COMMUNITY

Historically, church buildings have often been the center for religious ceremonies in the communities they served. Religious ceremonies include weddings, funerals, child dedications, baptisms, baccalaureate programs, Christmas Eve services, and other similar events. Small churches have historically hosted such events for the entire community, not just for the members of the church. There might have been limits to the types of ceremonies that each church was willing to sponsor, but in general, most community religious ceremonies occurred inside a church building.

As communities have become more postmodern, fewer people are coming to church than in the past. Some churches inadvertently contribute to the trend of postmodern people falling away from the church by enacting strict rules about who can participate in religious ceremonies that are held in their buildings. Such churches often fail to realize that many postmodern people still desire to take part in religious ceremonies even though they seem more distant from God than ever before. Though this may seem strange from an anthropological perspective, from a spiritual perspective, it makes perfect sense. God has designed us as spiritual beings made in His image.

Romans 8:29-30 says:

> For those He foreknew He also predestined to be
> conformed to the image of His Son, so that He would
> be the firstborn among many brothers. And those He
> predestined, He also called; and those He called, He
> also justified; and those He justified, He also glorified
> (NIV).

This passage indicates that God knew who would respond to
the gospel, and He has called those people to Himself. Therefore, it
makes sense that even though some people may have a postmodern
worldview, if God is calling them to salvation, there will be a God-
initiated desire in them for a relationship with God even though
they are not yet Christians. Their interest in religious ceremonies is
one piece of evidence that God is calling them to Himself. Healthy
churches are careful not to stand in the way of what God may be
doing. Church leaders would be wise to think carefully and pray
earnestly about how they can engage the next generation in as many
religious ceremonies as possible.

Allowing postmodern people who are not members of the church
to take part in some religious ceremonies of the church is important
because postmodernists see such ceremonies as important milestones
in their pilgrimage toward God. There often will be limits on which
religious ceremonies nonbelievers can take part in, but allowing
them to take part in some ceremonies inside the church building is
important.

For example, an evangelical church would not allow non-
Christians to be baptized, but they might allow them to have
a wedding or a funeral in the church building. Likewise, an
evangelical church would not want non-Christians to take
communion but might allow them to dedicate their children to
the Lord if they understand what they are doing. Church leaders
should consider the theological implications of allowing people
who are not yet Christians to participate in various ceremonies.
However, leaders should keep in mind that many postmodern

people will not choose to become Christians until they feel they are a part of the group.

Jimmy Long, a campus minister with InterVarstiy for over twenty years, has extensive experience working with young postmodernists. In his book *Generating Hope: A Strategy for Reaching the Postmodern Generation*, Long writes about the need for churches to help young people feel like they belong before they become Christians. Long points out:

> People today are more open than ever to hear God's Story because of the emptiness and brokenness of postmodern life. The Gospel story intersects with this generation's experience in a number of ways [including that] they feel unwanted and unneeded, [and] God's story offers them a place of belonging, a place for involvement, and a place where their lives can be used in service of a purpose that is larger than themselves.[1]

Churches that fail to help young people feel like they belong will eventually die. Referring to how important it is for churches to make young people feel like they belong, Ed Stetzer says that some churches are "dead for lack of friends."[2] These voices are calling for the church to throw open its doors and welcome nonbelievers to participate in various activities in the church. Churches will not always be able to say yes to postmodern people's desire to take part in religious ceremonies, but the more often churches can allow it, the more positively postmodern people will respond.

Church leaders might legitimately ask how allowing the next generation to take part in certain religious ceremonies is connected to helping postmodernists feel like they belong and thereby discover genuine faith in Christ. Dr. Wayne Oppel, who holds a doctorate in strategic leadership and has over thirty years of experience in leadership development, conducts workshops around the nation to help Christian leaders learn how to reach the next generation. He teaches workshop attendees:

The new theological thrust will be a return to the tradition of faith, especially the faith of classical Christianity expressed by the fathers of the church, the ancient ecumenical creeds and the practices of worship and spirituality found in the great traditions of the faith community.[3]

He goes on to elaborate that churches that want to reach the next generation will have to give "greater attention to the ritual as symbol, more attention to [religious] ceremony ... and more frequent celebration of the Eucharist."[4] As discussed in chapter 1, people with a postmodern worldview are looking for experiences. Religious ceremonies can provide those experiences. As church leaders spend time with young people helping them prepare for these experiences, they also build relationships. Real relationships combined with the experience of partaking in the ancient ceremonies of the church create powerful connections in the minds and hearts of the next generation.

The desire to belong does not necessarily mean that postmodernists want to join the church organizationally; it means they want to feel they are part of the group relationally. Henry Zonio, who is a staff member at Redwood Park Church in Thunder Bay, Ontario, explains it this way: "We turn church into a club with membership requirements, which if not met means exclusion from the benefits of being part of the club."[5] Zonio goes on to say:

> **The desire to belong does not necessarily mean that postmodernists want to join the church organizationally; it means they want to feel part of the group relationally.**

It is our job as citizens of the Kingdom to welcome people from all walks of life and at all points of their spiritual journeys into our communities. Doing that, though, takes risk. It takes willingness to struggle through the mess. It takes an unconditional love for people that goes beyond our preconceived ideas of what it means to be a part of a faith community.[6]

The decisions churches make about what types of religious ceremonies to allow outsiders to participate in often say more about the churches' commitment to evangelism than it does their theological positions. Finding that balance between theological integrity and intentional outreach can be a challenge, but it is a challenge worth engaging in.

Some churches may wonder if the next generation will just enjoy the benefits of using the building for religious ceremonies but never actually make a commitment to Christ or to the church. This is a valid concern. It is logical to conclude that some people will take advantage of the church. But the church has always had those in her midst who abused the care and compassion of the church for their own benefit. Why should we expect anything different from the next generation? Churches cannot allow the poor behavior of a few to keep them from attempting to reach an entire generation.

Postmodern people are looking for spiritual exercises that will actually help them find a meaningful relationship with God. Therefore, the vast majority of postmodern people are not interested in taking part in religious rituals that are empty or meaningless. They believe they can find a real relationship with God by taking part in the various religious ceremonies in the church, but those religious ceremonies must lead them to a deeper faith that has meaning and purpose.

The despair and confusion so prevalent among young adults can only be overcome by the power of Jesus Christ. As young adults experience Christ's love, He cleanses, restores, renews, and sets them on the right path. Preparing young adults to take part in various religious ceremonies is a perfect way to help them think deeply and contemplate spiritual issues. It is only through such deep thinking and inward reflection that they will find the spiritual strength they need to survive the harsh world that is now their constant reality.

Though a minority may take advantage of the church, this new generation of young people seems willing to think and reflect on a deeper level than the previous generation. While many members of the Great Generation were thinkers, the Baby Boomers were not nearly as deep. However, the grandchildren of the Baby Boomers are rediscovering the value of contemplation. The next generation is surrounded by difficulties and calamities at every turn. Family problems, financial difficulties, political turmoil, addictions, pornography, climate change, terrorism, and physical and sexual abuse are all issues that today's young adults deal with intellectually and emotionally on a regular basis. The difficulties they face may explain why so many young adults are filled with despair and confusion. It may also explain their desire to develop a spiritual dimension through meaningful religious ceremonies.

When church leaders do suspect a particular individual is only looking for a place for his or her ceremony and is not really interested in furthering his or her spiritual walk, those leaders must not be afraid to point out the fine line between deep spiritual contemplation and spiritual procrastination. Nothing is wrong with holding people accountable who are trying to gain access to spiritual benefits without accepting personal responsibility.

Some young adults have done enough contemplation to make a decision about spiritual things, especially if they grew up in even a nominally religious home. When we are preparing them to take part in religious ceremonies, we may discover they are unwilling to make a spiritual commitment precisely because they realize it will bring significant change into their lives. Even though they know they need to make that change and that the resulting change will have a positive impact on their lives, they are still hesitant to follow through on those commitments. At some point, their deep contemplation has become a smoke screen for spiritual procrastination. Such young people need to be challenged by a caring mentor. Part of the preparation process for participation in religious ceremonies must include time for such challenges.

It is important to point out that once postmodern people come to a committed faith in Christ, they are no longer content to sit and watch

> **Once postmodern people come to a committed faith in Christ, they are no longer content to sit and watch others lead religious ceremonies. They want to be involved in leading themselves.**

others lead religious ceremonies. They want to be involved in leading themselves. We are entering a time in church life when young adults desire to be leaders in the church, not just attendees.

The elders and deacons at Faith Community Church fondly recall one Sunday when the church was only about five years old. At that time, the youth had just begun to lead worship once a month. They were growing in their abilities. Their music was much edgier than the congregation was used to, but the leadership team wanted them to be involved, so the youth were allowed to lead. On that particular Sunday, nearly a hundred adults and their families worshiped to powerful praise music with hands raised and voices lifted as the youth band led the service.

Three rows of young adults were present in their customary section near the back. Halfway through the service, the youth praise team was singing a very upbeat song called, "I Am Free," by Jon Egan, who is the leader of a group called Desperation Band. The song was supposed to be what the church refers to as special music. That basically means the praise team was supposed to sing it on their own while the congregation listened. During the chorus of the song, suddenly those three rows of young people spontaneously rose to their feet and joined in singing the song with an enthusiasm they had never shown in church before. A wave of the Spirit flowed across the room, and the whole nature of the worship experience changed. For the first time, the youth band was actually leading worship and not just going through the motions. That particular group of young people has never been the same since. On that day, the congregation realized that God could use young adults in a powerful way even though it was different than the way worship was done previously. That youth band now leads worship regularly, and the congregation has gotten steadily younger, and quite a bit louder, as a result.

Many churches may think they need to allow young people to take part in religious ceremonies only so that they can build "the church of tomorrow." While church leaders mean well when they say things like this, what they are actually communicating to the next generation is that young people have no current value to the church. Young adults hear that message and decide that if they are not valued at church, they will go somewhere that does value them. Churches that do not value young people as the church of today should not be surprised when young people are not around tomorrow.

If churches want to attract younger generations, they have to begin to value them the way God does. Young adults need a real connection to Christ. They are often looking for a deeper spirituality than their parents have. When we help them prepare for religious ceremonies, they can discover the faith in Christ they need. Once they discover faith, we must let them lead. When we let them lead, they will set an exciting example for others to follow and draw their postmodern peers into the church as well. Churches must begin to recognize that young people are gifted by God and can be used by Him in powerful ways. Paul's exhortation to Timothy readily applies to young adults today: "Do not let anyone look down on you because you are young, but set an example for the believers in speech, in life, in love, in faith and in purity" (1 Tim. 4:12 NIV). Churches that can help the next generation live out that admonition will have no problem reaching people with a postmodern worldview.

CHAPTER FIVE

THE SMALL CHURCH FACILITY AS AN OUTREACH TOOL

Many small churches do not have all the space they desire, but they often have an advantageous physical location, such as at the center of the community or at a major crossroads. Such locations would be hard to acquire now but were often given freely to churches in the past. Churches that find themselves in a choice and advantageous physical location should use that location as an outreach tool. God put these churches in that location for a reason. While some small churches may be forced to close because they are not in good locations, most churches should consider their locations to be their primary mission field. Churches should re-examine why God placed them in the particular location with the particular facilities they have.

God's plan for world redemption includes using both the location and the facilities of a church to reach those outside the church, not just as a clubhouse for the current members. Churches that fail to take advantage of their location and facilities as an outreach tool will struggle. Churches that learn to use their location and facilities to their advantage will find it easier to reach newcomers to the community, as well as long-term residents who have adopted a more postmodern worldview.

If churches hope to use their buildings for outreach, the buildings should have curb appeal. Postmodern people have become used to living and working in a nice environment; therefore, if the church facilities look unkempt, then sophisticated postmodern people will drive right by. The church sign should be easy to read and have the main service times prominently displayed. Knowing what time the main services are scheduled is much more important to postmodern people than denominational affiliations, descriptive phrases about the church, or even the pastor's name. Though that information is important to church members, it is not very important to the next generation.

Some churches may struggle with this reality. Susan Brooks Thistlethwaite is the former president of Chicago Theological Seminary and currently a senior fellow at the Center for American Progress. Thistlethwaite reported in the *Washington Post,* "The religious landscape in the U.S. is best described these days as post-denominational. Post-denominational means that it is far less important whether you are Methodist or Baptist ..."[1] than in finding a church that works for you. She goes on to say, "When people move from one affiliation to another, they are choosing a better cultural fit" more than a new denomination to relate to.[2]

When postmodern people notice a church building exists in their community, they often see it as a place for more than just worship services. They see the church building as the perfect place for all kinds of community meetings that may have little to do with the formal ministries of the church. Churches have large rooms, such as the sanctuary or fellowship hall, for big group meetings, and they have multiple Sunday school rooms that can be used for small-group meetings. In many small communities, churches often have the best facilities for hosting community meetings.

Faith Community Church in Barre, Vermont, renovated a former commercial building to hold their worship services and outreach programs. The building was already handicap accessible, which made it ideal for use by community groups. Not long after moving into the building, a community organization that assists clients with brain injuries asked if they might use one room in the building three days a week. The church happily agreed, and as a result, many people have been in the building who otherwise may never have realized the church existed. One family that had been only nominally active became significantly more involved in the church because many of their friends were able to use that room over a period of several months. The husband eventually became a deacon because of their increased commitment to the church. Allowing the building to be used was also a great witness to many of the employees of that particular community organization.

Small churches across the nation often allow groups like the Boy Scouts or Alcoholics Anonymous to meet in their buildings. Many of these groups are often willing to make small donations to churches to help offset the cost of utilities. Each of these groups brings in a subset of people the church might never engage otherwise. Obviously, just having these groups meet in a church's building will not result in church growth if the members of the church do not interact with those using the facilities. But when church members make it a point to connect with these groups in a relational way, allowing community groups to use the church facility can become a powerful outreach effort. Small churches that are willing to consider as many ways as possible for the community to use their building for various events will increase the likelihood of new people coming to their worship services.

Postmodernists want a church building to be clean and fresh because they have become accustomed to such environments in their workplaces, schools, and homes, but they do not want to see a church building that is overly luxurious because it bothers them that money was spent on fancy buildings when there are so many poor people in the world. Churches should be careful about the use of ornate chandeliers and stained-glass windows or other displays of wealth that do not have a useful function. While a clean bathroom floor is essential, gold-plated faucets are actually a hindrance to reaching people with a postmodern perspective. Therefore, churches must think carefully about doing endless rounds of renovations to their buildings.

Incidentally, this same principle does not apply to extremely old church buildings. Postmodernists understand that in the past, many churches were built in a Gothic style. Somehow that does not bother them, and they view such an architectural style as a legitimate sacred space. If churches already own an older building with more ornate features, they do not need to get rid of them. But church leaders need to remember that postmodernists struggle to see the need for fancy new contemporary church buildings and additions that have an abundance of features for which there is no useful purpose.

Postmodern people expect lots of technology to be available in a church building. To them, projectors for PowerPoint presentations and screens for watching videos are standard items for any meeting. Though many small churches do not see the need for that level of technology, they might want to reconsider their views. Though small churches may be limited in how much money they can invest in technology at one time, it would be helpful for them to develop a technology plan and

> **Postmodern people expect a lot of technology to be available in the building.**

acquire what they need over time. Allowing that technology to be utilized not only in church services but also in meetings and events the community holds in the church building will speak positively to postmodernists.

Despite their size, many small churches are often blessed with good facilities. Though small churches may not have all the facilities they wish they had, they often have the perfect facilities for hosting community events. While there will obviously be some limits on the types of community meetings churches will be willing to host in their buildings, the more small churches can say yes, the better it will be for their growth. If small churches can keep their facilities looking nice without being overly opulent, if they can encourage community groups to use their buildings, and if they can engage those groups relationally, they may be surprised at how successful an outreach tool their buildings can be.

CHAPTER SIX

ENGAGING THE CULTURE
PHILOSOPHICALLY

With some modifications in how they function, many small churches can regain their position as the social, ceremonial, and physical centers of their communities. These adjustments will be relatively easy for small churches to make. Historically, small churches have also been the philosophical centers of their communities. In the past, people looked to churches for guidance, direction, and values. Though communities may have ideologically agreed with churches in previous generations, this is less true today. Small churches increasingly find themselves out of step with the postmodern worldview of their communities.

Churches that want to impact the changing values of their communities will require greater degrees of change than churches that just want to maintain the status quo. These changes will make many people uncomfortable. It is absolutely essential that pastors and church leaders approach change prayerfully and missionally if they hope to reach postmodern people without destroying their churches in the process. It is vital that whatever changes are adopted remain within biblical parameters. However, those changes will most likely be outside churches' traditional comfort zones. Pastors and church leaders can expect significant opposition from traditionalists within their congregations when trying to implement changes. That is why the philosophical area is the area where churches will have the greatest struggle to reach the next generation.

Many conservative Protestant churches have responded to the changing culture with a fortress mentality. Because these churches are determined to keep the changing culture out, they have encased themselves in a spiritual bubble that is rapidly shrinking. These churches refuse to consider any significant changes in methodology or practice, even though past methods and practices fail to communicate the gospel to the current culture. A number of recent surveys have shown young people are leaving those kinds of churches at an alarming rate. Researchers vary in the exact numbers, but most agree that between 61 percent and 88 percent of young people leave the church after high school and that only 35 percent return, usually around age thirty.[1] Churches cannot continue to pretend that everything is all right.

> **Many conservative Protestant churches have responded to the changing culture with a fortress mentality.**

Christians who hide inside religious fortresses often assume they are more spiritual than the communities around them. A growing number of individuals disagree with that assumption. Michelle Melecson[2] lives in southern Vermont. As a Christian, she is deeply committed to her personal faith in Jesus Christ and is active in a Southern Baptist church. Michelle also considers herself postmodern in her worldview and finds that she often relates to postmodern people better than to traditional conservative Christians. On her Facebook page, Michelle says, "I am a human, and so I fail. I am a Christian, and so I let God pick me back up again. I believe that the key to happiness is to figure out what gifts God has given you and then take those gifts and do great things with them." Michelle uses her gifts in a variety of ways but most enjoys working through civic groups that address specific needs in her community. She seldom sees churches meeting such specific needs, which is why she often serves the Lord outside the confines of the traditional church where she is a member. To Michelle, spirituality is about making a difference in the world, not hiding in a spiritual fortress.

Michelle surveyed some of her postmodern peers about their feelings about modern churches, and Michelle's friend Sheila said that some churches "feel more warm and inviting than other churches." The lack of warmth that some churches display makes it a struggle for people like Sheila to participate in church. Michelle's friend Becca said that in her experience, more than 50 percent of the churches she attended spoke "with empty hearts and empty minds, telling you to do this and that without any real commitment to what they are saying. They may talk the talk, they might even walk the walk, but they do not feel anything while they do it." That lack of passion is also a deterrent to postmoderns. If the church is not passionate about what it believes, why should postmodernists be? Becca went on to say, "Churches are supposed to have people in them acting as good role models. However, this is not the case most of the time." Like Michelle, Sheila and Becca are not convinced that everyone hiding behind the façade of religion is very spiritual. The fortress mentality adopted by some conservative Protestant churches is just not working. Such a mentality fails to communicate the gospel to postmodernists and also lacks warmth and passion, all of which are vital to reaching the next generation.

In the spring of 2009, I visited a rapidly growing church in Columbia, South Carolina, that was primarily attracting young adults to their worship services. It was an exciting experience that I wrote about on my blog (www.terrydorsett.com) the following week. My November 16, 2009, post included this section:

> Recently I was blessed to attend Midtown Fellowship Church in Columbia. This four-year-old congregation has several hundred young adults who attend one of five services each Sunday. At 42, I was clearly one of the "old people" in the group.

I watched as college students and young professionals worshipped God with passion. While their music was much more energetic than most churches, the focus of the music was on Jesus, not entertainment. I was amazed at how forcibly the congregation was challenged in a biblically based sermon to grasp God's concepts of stewardship and what that meant in the lives of those present. The preacher may have been dressed in blue jeans, but the sermon was not some watered-down version of the gospel, but a radical call to live like Jesus.

That blog post was re-published a few weeks later in the *Baptist Courier*, the official newspaper for the South Carolina Baptist Convention. Though many in South Carolina read the article and rejoiced that God was doing such a powerful thing among young adults in their area, two pastors wrote to say they disagreed with my observations. I encouraged them to visit that church for themselves and make their own observations. They replied that they did not need to visit the church because they knew all about "churches like that." Though I want to be careful not to judge my brothers in Christ, their comments highlight what I see as a disturbing trend developing in some traditional churches. I call it tradition idolatry.

Tradition idolatry is the tendency to assume that following one's religious traditions is the same thing as following God. Do not misunderstand. Many cherished church traditions are very meaningful, and it would be sad to see them neglected. But cherished traditions are not equal to biblical mandates. It is imperative that churches not give up biblical mandates, even though they may alter their manmade traditions multiple times.

> Tradition idolatry is the tendency to assume that following one's religious traditions is the same thing as following God.

Most traditions in churches were simply convenient ways to do things when the traditions were developed. Times have changed, but in many churches, the traditions remain. For example, many traditional churches have Sunday morning worship at 11:00 a.m., a time that worked well for the farmers who made up many congregations when the American culture was more agriculturally oriented. Today that particular time slot is not as convenient as it once was, yet the tradition remains in many churches. Churches that forget the point of worship, which is to honor and glorify God in spirit and in truth, and instead focus on the time slot are in danger of practicing tradition idolatry.

Perhaps the time slot is not important to some churches, but what about the instruments used in worship? Certain instruments were popular a generation ago, but different instruments may be popular today. The point is not the instruments themselves but how those instruments are used to glorify God. More-traditional churches may use a hymn book while less-traditional churches may project the words on the wall. Both are products of the times, and neither is mandated in Scripture. Congregations need to worship with a heart that is focused on God instead of on self. While traditions may have an aura of godliness, they are often simply catering to self because we tend to feel more comfortable with traditions. It is easy to confuse the feeling of comfort that comes with traditions with actual spirituality. When people choose to follow their traditions instead of following the Bible, the boundary of tradition idolatry has been crossed.

Just as manmade traditions can be obstacles to reaching postmodern people, so is theological liberalism. While conservative Protestant churches have often responded to the changing culture with a fortress mentality, many mainline Protestant churches have responded to the changing culture by essentially adopting postmodern values as their own. Thus, those churches have become increasingly more liberal in how they view Christian principles and values. Perhaps surprisingly to those congregations, this approach has seldom drawn in the community, and many mainline Protestant churches attempting to use this approach are still in steep decline.

Some of the reasons why congregations that choose to become more liberal still do not reach postmodern people are easy to understand; others are more complicated to sort through. Jay Guin, a lawyer from Alabama, who serves as an elder in the Church of Christ, has written two books on how that denomination is dealing with progressive cultural issues. He reminds churches, "Most of us don't leave our home congregation because change is so painful. But if the leaders make me endure painful change at my home church, I may decide to shop around because, well, I'm already in pain."[3] What Guin is trying to say is that many people will remain in the congregations they have been in their whole lives because it is too traumatic to leave, but if the values of those congregations change so much that it hurts even more to stay, then leaving becomes a more viable option. As mainline Protestant congregations have become more liberal, many of the longtime members have either moved to more-conservative churches or dropped out of church altogether. This has resulted in liberal churches becoming smaller instead of larger.

Paul Vanderklay, pastor of the Living Stones Christian Reformed Church in Sacramento, California, blogs regularly about how the liberal/conservative discussion is affecting the Christian Reformed Church of North America. In discussing what happens when a congregation becomes more liberal, he writes, "It's difficult when a denomination or congregation loses its conservatives, because conservatives often do more work and give more money."[4]

Regardless of what one thinks about theology or values, it is just a reality that the average conservative gives more money to charity than the average liberal. They also invest more time volunteering. That means that in most churches, the more conservative members are the backbone of those churches. When conservative members are removed, the churches lose their leadership, their volunteer labor, and their financial support. Even if a church adopting more liberal values attracted a small number of new members, often the number of older members who are driven away is even greater. It is important to note that we are talking about changing biblical values, not just adjusting programs, ministries, styles, or organizational structures. People will often endure stylistic, structural, or program changes, even if they grumble in the process. But when biblical values are discarded, that is often when the pain of staying becomes greater than the pain of leaving.

Many churches think the quickest way to attract younger people is to change the music style in the worship service. Guin notes, "I think we make a mistake in unduly focusing on instrumental music. It's an important issue, but it's not what's keeping us from growing."[5] The issue of music will be dealt with more fully in chapter 11, "What to Do When the Next Generation Finally Comes to Church." For the moment, just note that while music is an important issue, it takes more than just music to reach the next generation. We must actually be communicating truth to the

> **Anything built on something other than truth will eventually topple.**

next generation, whether it is in music, preaching, or interpersonal relationships. Anything built on something other than truth will eventually topple. Since postmodernists create their own truth, simply adopting their values will not help churches grow.

A second reason becoming more liberal does not work is that once they are removed from a biblical framework, these new values simply lack the ability to communicate biblical truth. The Southern Baptist Convention, America's largest Protestant denomination, has made a conscious decision to remain conservative and resist the liberal drift that many Protestant groups have made in recent years. Al Mohler, president of Southern Baptist Theological Seminary, one of the largest seminaries in the world and the flagship school for the Southern Baptist Convention, has addressed ways liberal denominations are trying to change. Mohler writes:

> The largest Presbyterian denomination, the Presbyterian Church, USA [PCUSA] has debated the same issues for years now, even as it has discussed allowing its clergy to replace references to the Father, the Son, and the Holy Spirit with metaphors like "Rainbow, Ark and Dove," "Speaker, Word and Breath," "Overflowing Font, Living Water and Flowing River," "Compassionate Mother, Beloved

Child and Life-Giving Womb," "Sun, Light and Burning Ray," "Giver, Gift and Giving," "Lover, Beloved and Love," "Rock, Cornerstone and Temple," and "Fire that Consumes, Sword that Divides and Storm that Melts Mountains."[6]

It is difficult for regular church attendees to understand these new metaphors because they are so abstract. Imagine how much more difficult it is for postmodern people, who have no biblical foundation, to grasp these confusing new religious metaphors. These metaphors are but one example of how theological liberalism leaves people confused. When churches cannot clearly communicate their message, it is understandable why fewer people attend. As fewer people attend, liberal churches seek to devise ever-more-complicated metaphors in the vain hope that one of those spiritual metaphors will connect with emerging generations. But the statistics reveal that mainline Protestant denominations continue to shrink rapidly, mostly because they have been unable to retain the church attendance of the next generation. What will be the end result of theological liberalism in these mainline denominations? Mohler concludes, "Short of a major act of God, mainline Protestantism will continue its slide into apostasy and irrelevance."[7]

While the pain that theological change causes and the confusion that liberal concepts bring are two major factors in why liberal churches continue to decline, the greatest reason lies in the fact that when the values of the church no longer stand in contrast to the culture, the church loses its identity and very purpose for existing. Vanderklay points out:

> Church growth pundits have long noted that groups that grow almost always have clear, specific, counter-cultural views that motivate their people to action."[8]

He adds:

> Part of the fatality of liberalism has to do with individualism. Deep in the heart of liberalism is the belief that ultimately I decide for me. [Since] ... churches are arrangements of convenience ... as soon as the cost-benefit balance tips out of my favor I'll seek out another convenience, or lifestyle that seems more "life giving" to me.[9]

In other words, once liberal churches lose the perceived value they added to individuals' sense of self, those individuals no longer see a reason to participate.

When churches become just like the culture, they are no longer counter-cultural. Consequently, they lose their appeal to younger generations who like to live on the edge. This is why churches want to engage the culture without actually adopting the culture. There is a huge difference between the two. Ignoring the culture is no longer an option; neither is adopting the culture. It is important for cultural issues to be understood and dealt with in a way that preserves biblical values if the church hopes to reach the next generation without losing itself in the process.

> **Churches will want to engage the culture without actually adopting the culture.**

Across the theological spectrum, others are reaching that same conclusion. Tony Robinson, president of the Seattle-based Congregational Leadership Northwest, speaks and writes, nationally and internationally, on religious life and leadership. The author of ten books, Robinson had a lot to write about in August 2010 when Mars Hill Church, which is a rapidly growing conservative church in Seattle, purchased the facility of a dying liberal church across town. While discussing why the conservative church was growing so rapidly while the liberal church had been in a long, slow decline, Robinson concluded:

> It may be that relatively comfortable liberals ... simply
> feel little need for religion. Meanwhile, the people
> Mars Hill is reaching may have experienced more
> of the rough edges of contemporary society and are
> receptive to a different direction.[10]

Robinson's writings hint at the idea that liberals just do not see the need for church involvement in their daily lives. Even as churches tried to attract postmodern people by becoming more liberal, they were chasing a fleeting fantasy because young people from that worldview were not interested anyway.

Jill Flannel[11] agrees with Robinson. Flannel grew up in a mainline Protestant denomination. Her husband served as a pastor in the denomination for more than twenty years, and she served as the women's ministry leader for the statewide organization of the denomination for many years. Flannel and her husband finally had to leave that denomination because of its continual slide toward theological liberalism. When asked why liberal churches in her former denomination were not growing, Jill responded, "If I'm OK and you're OK, why should we bother to get up on Sunday morning? We can watch Dr. Phil or Oprah and get the same stuff."[12] Jill has identified instinctively what Vanderklay and Robinson have concluded through research and observation. Pursuing liberalism as a means of church growth will not work because liberals do not think they need churches, regardless of those churches' theological beliefs.

Adopting postmodern values will not help to reach postmodern people. This method will not work because of the pain it brings to non-postmodern adults who are already in those churches. They will simply leave in greater numbers than postmodern young people can replace them. This method also will not work because it produces confusing religious symbols and metaphors that, once divorced from a biblical framework, fail to communicate significant spiritual truth to those seeking it. Finally, this method will not work because if churches adopt the values of the prevailing culture, then they lose their counter-culture identity and there is no point in being a part of a counter-culture movement that is no longer counter-cultural.

This leaves leaders of small churches in a predicament. If the fortress mentality will not work and if adopting postmodern values will not work, then what will work? The following chapters outline ideas and concepts that have been proven to work to reach the next generation. They will not be easy to implement, and wise leaders will move slowly, prayerfully, and in unison with other leaders. But the concepts that follow can be used effectively to reach young people with the gospel.

CHAPTER SEVEN

MOVING BEYOND THE WALLS OF THE CHURCH TO SERVE THE COMMUNITY

Postmodern people often lament that while the church talks about serving its community, such service to the community is actually rarely seen outside the four walls of the church. To reach postmodern people, Christians will joyfully practice outside the church building what is preached inside the church building. They will become involved in community organizations and activities that address real community needs. As churches and individuals move beyond the walls of the church to serve, they will intentionally take the gospel with them. Good deeds alone will not transform a community. A community can only be transformed as individuals within the community repent of their sins and place their faith in Christ. Therefore, missional activity can is only be considered successful if at some point people are called to repentance from sin and urged to place their faith in Jesus Christ.

Daybreak Community Church of Colchester, Vermont, has reached many postmodern people in their community of 17,237 by sponsoring community activities that meet real needs the church's members discover in the community. Since 2000, they have helped facilitate the annual Relay for Life event in their community, which raises funds and spreads awareness about cancer treatment. The church receives no direct benefit from sponsoring this event other than the goodwill of the community.

Daybreak has also helped with an annual summer marathon sponsored by the town. Their duties for the marathon include picking up all the rubbish left behind by the onlookers. This may not sound like a spiritual investment in the community, but as the community has seen the values of the church lived out in real life, they have responded well. Many previously unchurched people now worship regularly at Daybreak, where they hear a clear presentation of the gospel. These people would not have had the opportunity to hear the gospel if the church had not ventured outside its walls.

New Life Community Church in Northfield, Vermont, population 5,791, participates in their community's annual Labor Day celebration. While many other churches are selling pies and crafts to help fund various church functions, New Life sells lollipops to support the local Boy's Club. The community has noticed that New Life is helping others instead of only benefitting itself. At the celebration, church members also distribute hundreds of Frisbees with the gospel printed on them. Like Daybreak Community Church, New Life's members also help pick up rubbish after the two-day event is over. Also like Daybreak, the only benefit they receive from all this hard work is the goodwill of the community.

But that goodwill can go a long way. In December of 2009, a small church in Northfield closed. The leaders of that congregation had been so impressed with the way New Life was taking the gospel to the community that they felt led to give their building to New Life. They previously met in the local library and in various homes, so New Life gladly accepted the building and within a year had already filled that building to capacity.

Every small town has a community event that needs a sponsor, a school that needs painting, or a park that needs improvement. When churches take on such projects, they gain the attention of postmodern people and engage them at a deeply philosophical level. But to reach

> **Every small town has a community event that needs a sponsor or a school that needs painting or a park that needs improvement.**

these postmodern people for Christ, it is imperative that churches not shy away from proclaiming the gospel as they serve. It takes tact and common sense, but believers can effectively proclaim the gospel while serving others.

Closely aligned with a sense of serving the community is the idea of meeting the needs of those who are less fortunate. Even small communities have people who are hungry, homeless, and hurting. When churches demonstrate Christian love though compassion ministries, postmodern people take notice. Though churches will find a variety of ways to do this, every church should be involved in some way.

Barre Baptist Fellowship sits on a side street of Barre, Vermont (population of 8,837). In 1997 they started a soup kitchen to meet the needs of the homeless people they saw hanging out on a corner down the street from the church. Since then, their ministry to the homeless has grown to include serving nearly five thousand hot meals each year. The church also provides blankets, socks, and coats to the homeless during the winter months. The church often helps people find jobs and assists them with court hearings and legal proceedings. All of the compassion ministries Barre Baptist Fellowship sponsors are designed to help people hear the gospel and have an opportunity to discuss it with a member of the church. The congregation is now made up almost entirely of people who were reached through compassion ministries.

Churches from a variety of denominations in the area send volunteers and raise funds for the soup kitchen. Many young adults, especially college students, travel from around the country to assist the church in their ministry to the homeless and hurting. Because compassion ministries are very important to young people, they are willing to travel from around the nation at their own expense to assist in this ministry. Churches that reach out to young adults should expect them to want to get involved in such ministries. Though Barre Baptist Fellowship does not have many young people in its congregation, the church has been very instrumental in helping many young adults from other churches become more involved in their faith by helping the hurting.

David Russell serves as pastor of the Restoration Baptist Church in Burlington, Vermont. He is also the director of Burlington Street

Ministries. Since 1975 he has been serving the homeless on the streets of Burlington. Pastor Russell's congregation does not have a church building. The church uses homes of various church members for Sunday worship services. On Friday nights, Pastor Russell ministers out of a small push cart in the downtown area where the homeless frequently live. He holds Bible studies in the food court of a downtown mall and at a local McDonald's. He has even held Good Friday services in the alley between two downtown buildings.

Like Barre Baptist Fellowship, Pastor Russell utilizes many volunteers each year from both local churches and Christian college student organizations around the nation. Volunteers help him pass out Bibles and other Christian literature. They engage those they are ministering to in conversation. They distribute McDonald's gift certificates to those in need. They pray in the mall or on the streets with those who are troubled and looking for divine guidance. The many college groups who assist Pastor Russell are drawn to volunteer because, in their worldview, caring for the homeless is something Christians should be doing. Pastor Russell helps those who volunteer see the need to meet both the physical and spiritual needs of the homeless.

Helping the poor and oppressed is one thing postmodern people think Christians should actually be doing. Sadly, postmodern people seldom see evangelical churches serving in this manner. This inconsistency really bothers postmodern people. If churches want to reach postmodern people, churches will need to provide ways for young people to volunteer or otherwise support various ministries to the oppressed and downtrodden.

> **Helping the poor and oppressed is the one thing that postmodern people think Christians should actually be doing.**

Even if churches do not feel called to have a major compassion ministry of their own, it would be wise to find ministries at other churches to which they can channel volunteers and money. It is an oddity of postmodernism that by reaching out to the poor and downtrodden, churches can actually reach young professionals who are neither poor nor downtrodden.

Chapter Eight

Evangelism as a Process Instead of an Event

Some years ago, as we prepared to take part in a long-term mission assignment, my wife and I were required by the agency who was sending us to take part in a three-day evangelism training process. That evangelism process required us to memorize a fairly lengthy script that included spiritual questions people might ask, along with Bible verses to answer those questions. The process was very structured and worked well in the role plays we were required to do as a part of the training, but when we tried to use the method outside the training environment, it was not nearly as effective. In real life, the people we witnessed to did not ask many of the questions from the script. They also did not respond in the right way to the Bible verses we had memorized. I do not recall anyone ever making a solid commitment to Christ when my wife and I attempted to use that particular evangelism technique.

Since then I have learned a variety of other evangelism techniques. Though none were ever quite as much of a failure as that first method, none were ever as effective in real life as they seemed to be during the training process. I have come to believe that the problem with these various evangelism methods is that they all view evangelism as an event in which people say what is often referred to as the sinner's prayer. But if the people praying such prayers have no idea what kind of commitment they are actually making and do not have any desire to repent of their sins or live lives of service and devotion to God, then what value do such prayers have?

Postmodern people are on a spiritual journey; they are searching for truth. As a result, they view the search for truth as a process instead of an event. Because of that, they rarely respond positively to being asked to say a sinner's prayer after hearing a religious sales pitch from a well-intentioned Christian. While postmodern people may eventually say such a prayer, it will most likely occur after lengthy and thoughtful contemplation. If churches want to be effective in sharing the gospel with the next generation, they will view evangelism as a process instead of an event.

The truth of the gospel is going to be grasped one piece at a time by the next generation. The process is going to take longer than we want it to. Though the process may culminate in a precise moment where young people make deep commitments to Christ through prayers of repentance from sin and acceptance of Jesus as Lord and Savior, it will be the process itself that those young people will remember most and will refer back to as their journey to salvation.

One of the reasons the method of evangelism is important is that young people are not as interested in how many Bible verses Christians can quote as they are in how many biblical concepts Christians live out in real life. From a spiritual perspective, they need the truth of those Bible verses, but from an emotional perspective, they struggle to hear the truth until they see it lived out in the lives of others. Therefore, it takes time for Christians to prove the truth of their faith by living it consistently in front of postmodernists. As postmodern individuals see the truth lived out, they become more willing to hear the theological propositions that undergird the Christian faith. This requires an ongoing relationship between Christians and postmodern nonbelievers. Building these relationships takes far more time and effort than simply sharing a five-minute, memorized monologue on how to become a Christian.

This reality brings up one of the challenges of witnessing to the next generation: even though postmoderns desperately crave meaningful relationships, they also hesitate to form deep friendships because so many of them have been hurt in past relationships. Inwardly they desire to belong to something bigger and special. However, at the same time they fear being hurt, so they resist being connected to others to protect themselves from pain.

A couple of years ago, my wife and I were watching the movie *Into the Wild*, which is based on the life of Christopher McCandless, who traveled to Alaska and lived all by himself in an old school bus in the middle of nowhere. He thought he would be able to survive by himself without the companionship of other people. The movie portrayed a number of potential relationships McCandless resisted repeatedly. He walked away from those relationships because he was hurt in a close childhood relationship. That experience made him afraid to have another deep relationship. Regretfully, while hiking through the Alaskan wilderness, he accidentally ate a poisonous plant because he misread a guidebook, which led to his death a few days later.

If Christopher McCandless had other people with him, they might have noticed when he mistook a poisonous plant for an edible one. Perhaps they would have been able to help him hike back to town and seek medical help. Even if he felt he really needed some time alone, had he been willing to share his life with others, he could have told people where he was hiking so they could have come looking for him when he did not return. The story had a sad ending, but what made it even sadder was that it did not have to end that way. Christopher McCandless did not have to die isolated, alone, and far from home in an old school bus in the Alaskan wilderness. Ultimately, his distrust in relationships resulted in his untimely and tragic death.

In many ways, that is a picture of the lives of far too many postmodern people. Many of them have been hurt, and that hurt has caused them to emotionally isolate themselves from those around them. They think they can make it all on their own without other people and without God. Though they feel isolated and alone and deeply crave meaningful relationships, they fear further pain. As a result, they become paralyzed relationally. Though people of all ages need healthy relationships, the generation-long epidemic of broken families and the mobile nature of young adults have made this need more acute in the next generation.

God has designed us to need each other (1 Cor. 12). We need healthy relationships with others so we can experience the kind of life God wants us to have (Heb. 10:25). Even though we may experience some relationships that cause pain in our lives, we really cannot thrive without healthy connections to others. Even when we have been hurt by relationships in the past, those same relationships may give us hope in the future.

Consider Paul's experience in 2 Timothy 4:11 with Mark, a young man who caused him pain earlier in his life but who became valuable to him at a later date. Mark abandoned Paul at a critical time because the task ended up being harder than the young man originally thought. Paul persevered and successfully completed his mission without Mark's help. Later, when Paul planned a second effort, he refused to allow the young man to come with him. Paul's refusal created such a controversy that Paul ended up severing ties with some long-term ministry partners. But as time went by, Paul realized that Mark had matured and he needed that young man after all, even to the point of specifically asking for Mark to come help him. It was a risk because Mark could have abandoned Paul again, but Paul reached out anyway, and the relationship was restored. Relationships are always a risk, but they are a risk worth taking because life without relationships is less meaningful.

As we share our faith with others, we must be conscious of the fact that it takes time to build real relationships. It takes time to trust other people, but as we continue to live our faith in front of others and share what God is doing in our lives, God can use those relationships in wonderful ways. Christians need to take the initiative to build healthy relationship with others. Even though we may have been hurt in the past and we may be hurt again in the future, we must be willing to form meaningful relationships with others for our own relational well-being as well as for evangelism.

Another reason building relationships with young nonbelievers is an important part of evangelism is because postmodern people are often under the false impression that Christians live perfect lives. When young people build relationships with Christians, they discover that Christians have struggles too. When they realize that faith in Christ helps Christians to deal with those struggles, they become interested in learning more about Christ. When churches help their members engage in personal evangelism through sharing their own difficulties in life and how their faith gives them hope, it impacts the next generation deeply.

Faith Community Church in Barre, Vermont, has excelled in reaching troubled young people. One of the methods Faith Community Church has used is to have Christians share stories of their own struggles in life. The church has utilized interviews with young adults who grew up in difficult situations but found hope through Christ. Many of those interviews have been put on the local television station and recorded on DVDs and distributed to other young people. Some of those interviews have even been posted on YouTube. As young people see the power of the Christian faith to change people's lives, they become more interested in having that same kind of faith for themselves. Two words of caution are in order. First, when sharing our stories, we must be careful not to glorify the sin but to exalt the Savior. Second, we must also be careful not to fall into the "I versus you" syndrome.

For example, in the spring of 2010, I was taking part in a discussion group sponsored by a fairly traditional church in a nearby town. We were studying a powerful passage of Scripture I have enjoyed in the past. We were given a Bible study book that was published by a major Christian publishing house to use as a basis for the study. The leader of the group also shared stories of his journey of faith. Both the literature we were using and the leader's discussion of it were filled with statements like, "I did this and you need to do that too," "I stopped this behavior, and you need to stop this behavior too," and "You need to change the way you think, feel, act, and believe and become like me."

It became clear that the leader assumed the people in the discussion group could not possibly be living correctly until they changed their behavior to be more like his. After a while, both the study book and the leader's conversation became insulting. While I agreed that the leader had experienced a remarkable change in his behavior and I was in theological agreement with much of what he said, it was difficult to get past the constant "I versus you" statements.

The leader, perhaps unintentionally, seemed to imply that he had all the answers and had everything about life figured out. Postmodern young adults know better than that. Sharing our story in this way sounds arrogant and condescending to postmodern people. While it is important to share the stories of our own spiritual journeys when witnessing, churches that want to reach the next generation will teach their people to use we and us statements instead of I and you statements.

Using we and us statements helps young people feel as if they are part of the group instead of observers who are outside of the group. Since most postmodern people desire to belong to the group, when our witnessing methods create an artificial division between us and others, it can destroy that sense of belonging. Individual Christians, as well as religious teachers and preachers who want to connect with postmodern adults, need to retrain themselves to use statements that help people feel part of the group instead of being isolated from the group. This does not mean that we should not warn young people about dangerous or sinful behaviors; it just means that we should not create an "I versus you" environment in the process. Because young people will perceive this type of environment as being judgmental, they are unlikely to want to engage in a second dose of hearing how great Christians think we are.

Retraining ourselves to use we and us statements instead of I and you statements can be quite a challenge. The following might be an example of a less-effective statement: "If you continue in your addiction, you will never have a happy life. I trusted Christ, and it helped me overcome my addiction. I have

> **Retraining ourselves to use "we" and "us" statements instead of "I versus you" statements can be quite a challenge.**

been happier ever since. If you trust Christ, He will help you overcome your addiction, and you will be happier too." Though every word of the preceding statement may be technically accurate, to postmodern people it sounds arrogant.

An example of a more-effective statement might be the following: "Many of us have struggled with various addictions in our lives. We know what it is like to overcome such addictions, and we know what it is like to give in to those addictions. But as we have learned to turn from our sin and trust in Christ, we have found new strength to overcome our addictions. Let us encourage one another in our struggles and use the power of our faith in Christ to help one another overcome the addictions all of us battle." That type of statement expresses the need to turn away from sinful actions but does not put the hearer outside the group. To the contrary, it puts the speaker and the listener on common ground. Postmodern people will respond much better to this type of inclusive statement than to one with an I versus you perspective.

When we share our own faith journeys, one way to avoid displaying an I versus you attitude is to keep the focus on Jesus and how He changed us instead of on how we helped ourselves through willpower or positive thinking. Many people who do not consider themselves to be Christians still have a deep respect for Jesus. Therefore, they are interested in what Jesus did in our lives. Staying focused on Jesus is also more biblical. Jesus said in John 12:32, "As for Me, if I am lifted up from the earth I will draw all people to Myself" (HCSB). If we want people to come to Jesus, we need to lift up Jesus by focusing our discussions on Him. Though we may be sharing real stories of how Christ changed our lives, the focus will remain on Jesus, not on us.

Here is an example of a self-focused statement: "I was unfaithful to my wife on a number of occasions. I wanted to save my marriage, so I looked deep inside myself and saw a lot of attitudes I did not like. I began to work on those issues. I now have a much better relationship with my wife." Notice how often the word I is used and how God does not get any of the credit for the speaker's improved relationship with his wife? It gives the impression that the speaker did it all on his own.

A Jesus-focused statement might be something like this: "I was unfaithful to my wife on a number of occasions. The Lord began to deal with me about how He might help me save my marriage. Jesus began to show me a lot of stuff that was buried deep within me that had never been dealt with. As the Lord began to deal with each of these issues, my relationship with my wife greatly improved." This statement describes the same situation, but in this version, the Lord receives the credit for making the difference. In the first kind of statement, the speaker is taking the credit for himself. But if we were honest, we would have to admit that the second example is more realistic. We should give the Lord credit for doing His work in our lives. It is important when we are witnessing to share our journey of faith by focusing on how Jesus has helped us.

When witnessing to postmoderns, it is also helpful to talk about supernatural experiences we have had with God. In the summer of 2009, I had a conversation with a young friend who is agnostic. He wanted to know how I could be sure there is a God. Though he is still young, he is widely read and quite articulate about his agnostic faith. Though I could have given him a long list of Bible verses for why I believe in God, that would have been pointless since he does not accept the Bible as truth. There is power in the Word, so I wanted to share some Scripture with him, but I only shared two or three Bible verses that had special meaning to me. Then I went on to share a significant number of personal experiences I have had in my life that proved to me that God is real.

One example is what I call the green bean miracle. When I was a young father, my daughter pulled a pot of boiling green beans off the stove. She should have been horribly burned, but through God's power, the green beans landed in a circle around her body, with hot boiling water running all over the floor around her. Not a drop of boiling water or a single hot green bean landed on her. It was a miracle. It is scientifically impossible for such a thing to happen, yet it did. The green bean miracle is not a matter of faith because the experience actually happened. It is a historical fact. It is a real experience shared by my family. It is but one of many proofs of God's existence I have experienced in my own life.

Though only one supernatural experience would have been enough to prove God's existence, God has chosen to give me a long list of such experiences. Each experience reinforces the reality of God's existence in my mind. Postmodern people are very intrigued when I share such examples of God's activities in my personal life.

During a summer youth camp, I asked a group of young people if they had experienced any supernatural phenomena in their own lives. Most of the people in the group did not grow up in Christian homes, and very few of them were able to articulate their faith using theological terms. Yet one by one they shared stories of brain tumors shrinking, parents' marriages being put back together, victory over various addictions, and a variety of physical healings. Though some of them had not yet made commitments to become Christians, the vast majority did believe there was a God because of their supernatural experiences. Those experiences are part of the process postmodern people work through in their journey toward Christ. It is important to note that supernatural experiences alone are unlikely to result in a solid commitment to Christ, but when they are coupled with a powerful Scripture or two, they speak volumes to postmodern young people.

Squire Rushnell has gathered stories of these kinds of experiences across America in his book *When God Winks*. He calls these experiences Godwinks. Rushnell believes that when we have an experience that can only be described as supernatural, it is actually God winking at us to remind us that He is there and He is involved in our lives. Rushnell is a veteran ABC network television executive whose leadership saw the *Good Morning America* program rise to number one in its time slot and its ratings increase by 140 percent. He also developed the acclaimed *Schoolhouse Rock* series and the ABC After-School Specials, which earned seventy-five Emmy Awards during his career. He left that lucrative and powerful career to travel the nation sharing how we can know for sure that God is real because of the Godwinks that happen to us regularly.[1] Books like Rushnell's can be powerful witnessing tools to help postmodernists realize that God is real and He wants to be involved in our lives.

We must remind young people that there is a fine line between genuine miraculous experiences and slippery con artists. The media tends to promote the more bizarre experiences and often ignores the smaller Godwinks that are happening all around us. Yet these smaller Godwinks that happen on a regular basis are more important in displaying the existence of God than some of the more bizarre reports that make it on the news.

As our culture has become more secular in nature, many people feel less connected to the divine than they once were. This sense of disconnection causes great anxiety for many people because deep down inside, we know that something is "up there somewhere." This sense that something bigger than us is out there fuels postmodern spirituality. This should not be surprising since God is the one who put eternity in our hearts (Eccles. 3:11).

However, knowing that something is up there somewhere is different than actually knowing Christ in a personal way. As Christians, we must at some point actually share the gospel with our postmodern friends. When that moment comes, we must make sure we do not undermine all the hard work it took to move through the process. During the long process of evangelism, and especially as we finally arrive at the culminating moment of our witnessing efforts, we need to remember several practical items to be effective in our witnessing.

First, we may want to consider using a version of the Bible people can actually understand. Because many postmodern people have a minimal understanding of the Bible, using a version they cannot understand only complicates the situation. Because of this, it can be beneficial to let go of our own personal preferences and use a version of the Bible the next generation can understand.

Second, we should ask open-ended questions instead of making declarative statements. Open-ended questions are ones that cannot be answered with a yes or a no. Open-ended questions invite discussion. When we ask questions that have a yes or no answer, we tend to lapse into presentation mode, which is often perceived as nonauthentic.

> **Open-ended questions invite discussion.**

Presentation mode tends to answer questions people are not asking and miss the issues they really want to discuss. When our friends are finally ready to have the big talk about salvation with us, it will be a two-way discussion, not a one-way lecture. Asking open-ended questions helps us keep the conversation going.

Third, we should be prepared to admit that we do not know all the answers. The person with whom we are sharing our faith may ask complex questions. These questions will often be based on negative experiences they have had or some evil they have seen in the world around them. We may not know the answers, and there may not be any answers. It is fine to admit that we are still looking for answers to those questions ourselves. Admitting that we trust Christ even when we do not know the answers is a powerful testimony about the depth of our faith.

Fourth, we must realize that the results of our witnessing will depend on the Holy Spirit. Sometimes we push too hard when we witness because we think we are the ones responsible for other people's souls. We are only responsible for sharing the gospel. God is responsible for the results.

Though sharing our faith with postmodern people is a challenge, Christ commands us to share His love with others, and people need the comfort and hope that faith in Christ gives. Postmodern people do not deserve an eternity of separation from God simply because witnessing to them is a challenge. We can overcome the challenges of witnessing to the next generation when we realize that it is more a process than an event. Part of that process involves building healthy relationships with the next generation. Part of the process includes retraining ourselves to use we and us statements instead of I versus you statements when we tell the story of our own struggles toward faith. Part of that process includes focusing on Jesus and how He changed us during our struggles instead of pretending we did it all on our own. Another part of the process includes talking about the supernatural experiences we have had in our lives. Finally, the process concludes with leading our friends to new faith in Christ. If we stumble on that last point, the whole process will have been in vain.

Chapter Nine

Helping a Generation in Pain

When we begin the process of sharing our faith with the next generation, one of the first obstacles we will encounter will be the deep pain young people have observed in the world around them and experienced in their own lives. They want to know why God allows all this pain if He is so loving, kind, and powerful. They want to know why God does not use His power to stop all the pain. They frequently ask, "If God really loves us so much and has so much power, then why do bad things keep happening to us?" This question has been asked countless times by both adults and young people through all generations, but it is particularly being asked by postmodernists. Because we who are Christians have probably asked this question ourselves on more than one occasion, we can relate when young people express their struggles through this question. It is not an easy question; there are no easy answers. Trite phrases and platitudes will not suffice. Our response should include great gentleness and wisdom because the pain of the next generation is a significant issue.

Facebook has become a very effective tool for counseling the next generation. I spend a lot of time talking to young people through this medium. In my discussions with

> **Facebook has become a most effective tool for counseling the next generation.**

these young people, they feel comfortable sharing about their hurt and pain because they can hide behind their computer screens or their smart phones. Young people have shared with me about their broken and dysfunctional homes that have caused a tremendous amount of sadness in their lives. They have shared about losing friends in various types of tragedies. They have shared about beloved grandparents suffering horribly from cancer or some other illness and then slowly dying. They have shared about being betrayed by good friends or close relatives. They have shared that they were violated sexually by an older friend or relative. Considering the level of pain and hurt the next generation has already experienced, it is a wonder that any of them function at all.

This pain became even more evident to me at a large youth rally at a church in our area where I spoke in January 2009. Though I did not know everyone who was there, I knew enough of them to know it was a room full of pain. Many of the young people who were present were from broken homes. Many were from families that faced significant financial challenges. At least five young people present had lost one parent to death, two only forty-eight hours before the rally. Teenagers were present who had been physically and/or sexually abused.

One young man present had been bounced from house to house, never quite knowing where home was any particular week. Several dozen had lost friends in car accidents, one only a few weeks before. Others present at the youth rally had lost friends in a horrific house fire that took several lives, and some had lost friends in a freak drowning accident in a normally calm river that ran through the middle of our town. Several of those present were struggling with addictions in their own lives or in the lives of their parents. The group also included at least two cutters (people who intentionally cut themselves so their body will release natural endorphins that make them feel better) and at least three who were struggling with their sexual identity. As I prepared to speak to the group, I could feel the intensity of the group's pain.

My experience when speaking to that group reinforced in my mind that the next generation is a generation that is in pain. Not only are they dealing with significant emotional issues, but they are also the first generation that will most likely be less well off than their parents. They are inheriting an economy that is in shambles, a morality that has collapsed, and a nation that has lost status on the global scene. With so much stacked against them, the last thing young people need is churches that do not care about their pain or help them with their struggles. Yet that is what many young people find when they occasionally wander into church.

Based on my experience ministering to so many young adults, it has become clear that many of them blame God for the pain in their lives. Some of them do it outright and boldly, expressing great anger at God for letting bad stuff happen to good people. Others are more subtle, but they clearly question why a God of love would let bad things happen. God takes the blame for every painful moment and every painful action that has ever occurred in their young lives and in the world around them. If we church leaders want to reach the next generation, we are going to have to help young people deal with all this pain, along with the anger that emerges from it.

Three primary causes of pain exist in the world. The first cause of pain is our own sin. God has declared certain behaviors to be sinful. Because postmodern people struggle with the concept of absolute truth, they will struggle to accept that there are certain behaviors that are sinful. Though postmodernists may struggle with the concept, that struggle does not negate the reality that certain actions are wrong. Though some people may feel God's declarations about sin are arbitrary, that is not the case. God has declared certain actions to be sinful because of the great pain those actions cause either in our lives or in the lives of others.

Just as God has declared certain actions to be sinful, He has also declared certain attitudes and behaviors to be right. Right behavior brings more health and happiness and less pain into our lives. Wrong behavior steals our happiness and creates greater pain in our lives.

Committed Christians accept these declarative absolutes. We read about them in the Bible and seldom question why they may be right or wrong. We just try to follow them the best we can. But postmodern people are not going to accept right and wrong without asking questions about why those actions are right or wrong. Churches often do not know how to respond when young adults question what the Bible says about sin. One way to respond to these questions is by showing the connection between sin and the pain that results from sin. We can help postmodern people realize that God is not a cosmic killjoy who is trying to keep us from having fun. God is a loving Father who is trying to keep us from hurting ourselves or others.

I met Sahara[1] shortly after she moved to our area. Though she was not religious, she heard about our church and thought it would be a great place to meet new friends. Sahara is quite outspoken in her opinions on many things, including her lifestyle choice of lesbianism. She is a leader in a pro-lesbian group that is sponsored by a local organization. She makes no secret of her feelings on that issue or a host of others. Sahara's strong opinions often result in her making many poor decisions, which have had an adverse effect on her relationships and her sense of well-being. Her choices have caused a great deal of pain in her life, but she is so confident that she is right that she seems incapable of changing course so her life can have less pain.

Her pro-lesbian group told her this pain was caused by the narrow-mindedness of others. They told her that if her family and friends would just accept her lesbianism, then she would feel better about herself. Sahara has worked hard at pressuring those around her to accept her lifestyle choice. Many have done so, but she is still miserable, which demonstrates that others' acceptance of her choices will not end her pain.

At one point Sahara's many issues compounded themselves so much that she could barely function. One evening after church, she began to talk about why she so badly needed us to accept her sexuality. I had heard her repeatedly share her opinions on the matter, so I decided it was time to confront her about her choices. I explained, with as much love as I could, what the Bible says about her choices—not only about her lesbianism but about a number of other negative choices she regularly made.

The conversation got very tense. She said she did not think she could come back to a church that did not accept her the way she was.

As gently as I could, I told her that we did accept her as she was, but we loved her too much to leave her as she was. I pointed out that she did not seem very happy the way she was, and it would be wrong of us to ignore her deep pain. I suggested that much of her pain was a result of something being wrong inside her, which the Bible identifies as sin.

Sahara got defensive and left angry. We did not see her at church for a couple of weeks. But then she came back. She declared that she was going to work on all of her problems and try Bible reading and prayer. After several more weeks, she declared herself a "half-Christian." By that she meant that she now believed there was a God, but she was not quite ready to commit to Him. God is doing a deep work in Sahara's life. God is showing her a way out of pain, but it requires her to make changes in many of her lifestyle choices. The method I used with Sahara was to show her the connection between her poor life choices and the pain she was experiencing. By using this method, I was able to help her understand that I was not trying to judge her but to help her out of her pain. It has taken a long time, and the process is not yet finished, but I am confident that He who began a good work in Sahara will complete it when the time is right (Philippians 1:6).

As I minister to young people, they often ask me why God gives us so much freedom to make such choices if we are just going to make choices that cause us pain. Young people want to know why God did not make us in such a way that we will always do what is right. This is a complicated question. The answer focuses on the free will God gives to people.

I try to help young people understand that though God is indeed all powerful and could control our lives so we would be free from all pain, that choice would render us mere robots or puppets on a string that God was dangling around in the world. God loves us too much to give us such empty and meaningless lives. God has chosen to give us free will as an expression of His love for us. Unfortunately, our free will has been deeply tainted by our fall into sin.

The apostle Paul confessed in Romans 7:15, "For I do not understand my own actions. For I do not do what I want, but I do the very thing I hate" (ESV). This verse shows that even Paul struggled with his free will and its tendency toward sin. Free will has a price, for with control comes responsibility. Much of the time when we think we are exercising our free will, we are actually acting as slaves to our sin.[2] This slavery to sin causes part of the pain we experience in our lives. Pain is often the natural consequence of our bad choices. When we trust Christ as our Savior, we are freed from our slavery to sin. We receive the Holy Spirit, and He helps us make better choices and use our free will as God intended it. When we use our free will as God intended, it has positive results. When we use our free will in a way that God did not intend, the consequences are almost always painful. While we are free to make our own choices, we are not free to choose our own consequences.

Many people prefer to make bad choices and then blame God for the results of those choices, but that is just not the way the real world works. Everyone wants God to fix their problems, but no one wants to join God in His efforts to do the fixing. God is always at work to bring hope to the hopeless and to change painful situations into joyful experiences. Hope and help are gifts from God, who is both powerful and loving. But we must respond to Him when He reaches out to us. We must open our hearts and minds to His working in our lives. If churches hope to help postmodern people come to faith in Christ, churches will work hard at expressing love to those who are bound up in sin while patiently showing a biblical way out of the pain sin causes.

> **Many people prefer to make bad choices and then blame God for the results of those choices.**

If we think through the concept of free will completely, we have no choice but to conclude that though God is able to free us from all the pain of life, that would be inconsistent with His gift of free will. Therefore, one reason life can be painful is that even though God has given mankind the ability to make choices, mankind has not used that ability very well. We have used our free will to sin, and that sin has caused much of the pain in our lives. This may not be politically correct in our pluralistic culture, but it is morally, theologically, spiritually, and emotionally correct. We must help the next generation understand the connection between sin and pain.

While our own sin nature and our wrong choices are root causes for pain and suffering in our lives, the second cause for pain in the world is the sin of others. Sin has a ripple effect that causes pain to other people. Sadly, even when we trust Christ and He frees us from the grip of our sin, we are still subject to the poor choices others make who are still in slavery to their sin. As a result, we also experience pain when others make bad choices, and their consequences spill over into our lives. Sometimes the people hurt the most by sin have no direct connection to the individuals who actually commit the sin.

There are countless examples of the sin of others having huge impact on people with no direct connection to the sin. I still remember the horrifying pictures of Bhopal, India, on the news on December 3, 1984. I was a senior in high school at the time. Over a period of several days, nearly half a million people in Bhopal were exposed to the toxic gas Savin, which had leaked from a nearby pesticide plant. According to *Earth Magazine*, "Approximately 3,800 people died immediately. Thousands more died in the coming days. Those who survived recovered slowly or not at all."[3] What caused this terrible leak? Workers at the factory claim that the plant's "owners were known for their lax safety standards."[4] Having low standards was a way to save money and increase profits. The company denies this claim, but records indicate that "the safety systems that should have kicked in ... weren't working properly."[5] This was one of the worst industrial accidents in history. Whether it was caused by the sin of greed or by the sin of laziness, either way, the sins of a few caused unbelievable pain to many people who had no direct connection to the people who sinned.

This whole process of the sins of one person hurting another began with Adam in Genesis 3. When Adam sinned, the perfect world God created became tainted by sin. One result of the taint of sin was natural disasters. Such disasters cause significant pain to the lives of millions of people who never even knew Adam existed. The ripple effects of Adam's sin continue to cause pain to people after many millennia. In the past most people were not aware of the pain that natural disasters caused around the world. Today, through the Internet, cable television, and other technological advances, the next generation has witnessed dramatic suffering in the world that was not caused by the people who experienced the pain. The terrible tragedy of 9/11, the tsunami of 2004, and the earthquakes in Haiti in 2010 and in Japan in 2011 are but a few examples of pain the next generation has seen. They have been victims of significant pain themselves—pain they did not cause. Even when they accept the fact that some of their pain was self-inflicted, they still want to know why God did not stop the pain that others caused and why God did not stop the pain that results from natural disasters. That is why it is important to have conversations about free will. Just as we have misused our free will, others have misused their free will as well. That freedom may cost other people dearly. Adam used his free will to bring the curse of sin on the world, which is a constant reminder of how far reaching one person's freedom might be. While it is tempting to ask God to let us keep our free will but limit the free will of others, we know that is not realistic. Young people must be reminded of this reality on a regular basis.

A word of caution is in order. While some of the pain in our lives comes from the sins of others, we must not allow that to become an excuse for developing a victim mentality. Second Timothy 1:7 says, "God gave us a spirit not of fear but of power and love and self-control" (ESV). Christ came so we could find the strength to overcome the troubles of this world. Churches need to help young people understand that while some pain is caused by the sins of others, we can overcome that pain through our faith in Christ. We do not have to live in fear. We may have been victims in the past, but through Christ, we can find victory over a victim mentality.

The third cause of pain is Satan. God is not the only spiritual force at work in the world. Satan loves to cause pain. Satan is roaming about the world with his legions of demons looking for those he can destroy. First Peter 5:8 says, "Be sober! Be on the alert! Your adversary the Devil is prowling around like a roaring lion, looking for anyone he can devour" (HCSB). Satan is the one who kills people in car accidents and house fires. Satan is the one who causes one person to violate another person sexually. Satan is the one who delights in bringing cancer, disease, and pain into the world. We need to put the blame on Satan, where it belongs.

Consider Adolph Hitler. Though he was a relatively obscure politician with poor writing skills, he somehow managed to capture the attention of an entire nation. He then used that platform to promote unbelievable evil, resulting in the death of millions of people. How did he manage to convince a whole nation of intelligent, well-educated, and morally upright people to support so much evil? Clearly there was a spiritual force behind him—but it was a spiritual force of evil. Many older people who look back on some of Hitler's methods now recognize occult-type rituals and practices Hitler used to consolidate his power. The root of his power was beyond his personality; it was in Satan. We must never forget that, or else that terrible scenario could be repeated somewhere else in the world.

Hitler is not the only example of demonically inspired evil. I have read accounts of serial child molesters who described an evil power that overtook them when they would do terrible things to innocent children. Serial killers have similarly described a feeling of an overpowering force that compelled them to murder their innocent victims. Normal people do not engage in such aberrant behaviors. When people do things that evil, there is likely a supernatural force behind their actions.

The next generation needs to be taught how to do spiritual battle with Satan. Ephesians 6:12 teaches, "Our struggle is not against flesh and blood, but against the rulers, against the authorities, against the powers of this dark world and against the spiritual forces of evil in the heavenly realms" (NIV). Young people need to know how to recognize Satan's efforts and overcome Satan's power through faith in Christ. First John 4:4 says, "For He who is in you is greater than he who is in the world" (ESV). We can overcome Satan's efforts, but we must be focused and intentional in our battle against him. This does not mean that Satan will never bother us again. Satan will continue to do evil because he is pure evil and does not know how to do anything but cause pain and hurt in the world. Christians, however, have the power to stand against Satan.

Much of the pain in our world is caused by sin. Sin really does hurt us, whether it is our sin or the sin of others. Satan is real and is working hard to hurt people as well. Though some people may not want to admit it, faith really does help us find relief from pain and discover happiness and joy in our lives. In fact, our past pain can help us assist others who are going through similar types of pain. The apostle Paul talks about this in 2 Corinthians 1:3-4:

> Blessed be the God and Father of our Lord Jesus Christ, the Father of mercies and the God of all comfort. He comforts us in all our affliction, so that we may be able to comfort those who are in any kind of affliction, through the comfort we ourselves receive from God (HCSB).

Paul is reminding us in this Scripture that our own pain can be used by God to comfort other people who have experienced similar pain. However, for that to happen, we have to know God and trust that He works through the painful experiences in our lives to bring about the ultimate good. When we realize that, our past pain can become a powerful ally to help others. It is the comfort that we draw from our faith that helps us overcome pain in our lives. Those who have no faith must endure the same pain as everyone else but without the help of God. Young people need to realize that life is better when God is involved.

Not long ago I had an Internet-based debate with a group of spiritual skeptics from Arizona State University. They asserted that people who are religious are emotionally unhappy and mentally unhealthy because of the great sense of guilt religion unfairly places on people. They thought all this talk of sin and Satan is proof that faith is more harmful to people than helpful. I challenged their assumptions based on my own life experiences and on Scripture, but they insisted they were right. They said they had facts to prove their claim was correct. I asked them to produce their evidence. Despite their adamant insistence, they were unable to cite a single scientific study or survey that backed up their outrageous claim that faith hurts instead of helps. Most of the arguments those students made came from Christopher Hitchens' book, *God Is Not Great: How Religion Poisons Everything.* Hitchens has become a hero to many young people who want to blame God for all the pain in their own lives and in the world around them.

Since those ASU students had no facts to support their claim that faith hurts instead of helps, I decided to do my own research on the subject. I was amazed at how much evidence exists to verify that faith is a positive influence in our lives. WebMD.com reports:

> People who attend religious services, or who feel they are spiritual, experience lower levels of depression and anxiety; display signs of better health, such as lower blood pressure and fewer strokes; and say they generally feel healthier.[6]

That same website revealed that not only are religious people healthier, but they also live longer. In a study of over four thousand people, Dr. Harold G. Koenig, of Duke University Medical Center in Durham, North Carolina, reported, "People who attend religious services at least once a week are less likely to die in a given period of time than people who attend services less often."[7]

Dr. Michael Roizen and Dr. Mehmet Oz reported similar findings in a recent article entitled "Feel the Spirit." In that article, the doctors reference a "study of 6,534 older Chicago residents, who said they have spiritual experiences every single day."[8] The study revealed that going to church "can protect against age-related memory loss and thinking problems."[9] It went on to say, "People who go to services more than once a week have half the risk of major depression as those who attend less often."[10] Researchers at Florida State University found that "regular prayer increases your concern for other people ... that could help you make your part of the world a brighter, better place."[11] A number of other studies made similar conclusions, and a simple Google search will reveal them to anyone interested in checking out those claims on their own.

The research clearly shows that religious people are healthier and live longer, but are they actually happier? In 2009 Professor

Andrew Clark, from the Paris School of Economics, and co-author Dr. Orsolya Lelkes, from the European Centre for Social Welfare Policy and Research, examined numerous surveys and scientific studies done in Europe and concluded that deeply religious people have higher levels of life satisfaction than nonreligious ones.[12] Clark and Lelkes concluded that religion in general acts as a buffer that protects people from life's disappointments.[13]

The connection between happiness and faith is not just true for our European friends. The highly respected Pew Research Center discovered that in America:

> People who attend religious services weekly or more are happier than those who attend monthly or less; or seldom or never. This correlation between happiness and frequency of church attendance has been a consistent finding for years.[14]

Two studies led by psychology professor Michael Inzlicht at the University of Toronto reveal that believing in God can help block anxiety and minimize stress.[15] In October 2010, three researchers from Princeton, New Jersey, reported:

> A new analysis of more than 550,000 Gallup-Healthways Well Being Index interviews conducted over the last year and a half finds that Americans who are the most religious also have the highest levels of wellbeing.[16]

For those who may think that the link between faith and wellbeing is just a coincidence, researchers report, "The difference in wellbeing between the religious and nonreligious populations is highly statistically significant given the large sample size this research uses."[17] The bottom line is that faith simply makes people happier. Faith can help us deal with the pain in our lives, regardless of the source of that pain.

People who are deeply religious do not need a survey to tell them they are happier than their nonbelieving friends. They already know this because they witness it on a regular basis. That does not mean that religious people do not have bad days or have periods of time in which they may feel depressed, but it does mean that as a general rule, they live happier lives than those who are not religious. This may not be politically correct in today's pluralistic culture, but it is scientifically accurate. Though some people may not like religious faith, there is simply no denying that faith improves people's quality of life. We may all be entitled to our own opinion on the subject, but we are not entitled to our own facts. The facts are clear: religious faith makes us healthier and happier and increases longevity.

When postmodern people find themselves involved in unhealthy activities and poor lifestyle choices that lead them to significant amounts of personal pain, they need someone to show them a better way to live. This means that churches need to find ways to gently connect sinful behaviors that cause the pain that naturally results from those behaviors. In the past, people just took the church's word that certain actions or behaviors were sinful and tried to steer clear of those things to the best of their ability. But since postmodern people decide what truth is based on their own research and experiences, they are likely to have to learn about the consequences of sin by experiencing them personally.

Once young people become involved in sinful behavior and begin to feel the pain of their bad choices, they may be more open to understanding the truth of the gospel. Young people often show up at church because of deep pain that was the result of sinful actions. It is in that moment of crisis that someone should reach out to them and offer a way out of pain. But the church often rejects these young people who are searching because of their behavior just when postmodern people need Christians the most. It is easy for biblically minded Christians to forget to express the love of God while also exposing sin for what it is. Churches that can find the right balance between expressing love and pointing out how much sin hurts will connect well with postmodern people.

Postmodern young adults who live in a culture of brokenness are looking for something that can ease their pain. Churches can help postmodern young people understand the hurt that is caused by bad choices. Young people are not interested in hearing about a fairy-tale world where people just say a prayer and all their problems go away. They know that world does not exist. Instead they need to hear about our own spiritual journey with all its bumps, setbacks, troubles, and hardships. They need to hear about the times we doubted and were afraid. They also need to hear that we received the strength we needed from our faith to keep going despite our troubles. They need to know there is hope to be found through faith in Jesus Christ.

The day of free pizza and having a fifteen-minute feel-good devotional as a way to reach young adults is over. Today churches that want to minister to young adults had better plan for lengthy discussions that will not have simple conclusions or easy answers. That does not mean young people no longer like to eat pizza. It just means that free pizza will not satisfy the deep longing young adults have for answers to the complex world into which they have been thrust. Churches willing to invest the necessary time, energy, and love into the lives of young adults and journey with them through the difficult questions and experiences will find those young adults quite interested in what churches have to say.

If churches fail to help young people deal with pain, those churches should not be surprised when the next generation looks for comfort in other places. Churches have been called to hold the keys to the kingdom of God. Too many churches have lost the keys. It is important for churches to rediscover those keys before they lose a whole generation. One of the ways churches can rediscover the keys to the kingdom and unlock spiritual truth for young people is to help them deal with the pain they have experienced in life and the evil they observe in the world around them. Fortunately, the Bible is filled with practical advice about these subjects. If churches can communicate these biblical truths in ways the next generation can understand, they will find ears eager to listen.

CHAPTER TEN

HELPING NONBELIEVERS SEE THE LOGICAL PATH TOWARD A GOD OF TRUTH

While many young people blame God for the pain in their lives, others have decided that God does not exist. Many of those who have chosen not to believe in God have become quite evangelistic in their anti-God rhetoric, using YouTube videos, seminars, blogs, and books that bolster their anti-God stance.

After having read several books written by authors who seek to deconstruct Christianity,[1] I have noticed a number of similarities in them. The first is that several of the authors had had a connection with a more formal or liturgical church during their childhood but dropped out of church in their teens or early adult life, primarily because that highly structured and often overly ritualistic church experience did not meet their spiritual needs. They falsely equate their personal church experiences with God. They also falsely believe that their church experience is the norm for all churches. They theorize that since their church experience was not relevant to their worldview, then God must not be relevant. They assume that churches, and by extension, God, cannot meet the spiritual needs of postmodern people.

These writers are convinced that their negative personal experiences with religion somehow negate the positive personal experiences of hundreds of millions of Christians around the world. They are also convinced that since they have concluded that churches and God are both irrelevant to life, then God must not exist, and it would be acceptable to them if churches did not either.

Another similarity is that these writers find extreme examples of religious abuse and then try to make the case that the extreme is actually the norm. For example, many of them will refer to violence that has happened somewhere in the world due to religious extremism. Then they wrongly conclude that all religious people are prone to violence.

This could not be further from the truth. This approach ignores the reality that the vast majority of the followers of all religions are nonviolent. There will always be a small group of people who are willing to use religion to force their will on others. That has nothing to do with religion and everything to do with those individuals' quest for power. Those same types of people will also use money, politics, education, or the legal system to force their will on others. Their quest for power is what fuels their fervor, not their faith.

Another similarity is that these authors omit any discussion of the weaknesses of nonreligious people. They will discuss in great detail the violence of a handful of religious extremists, but they fail to mention the violence of atheist governments such as China, Cuba, or the former Soviet Union. These nations did terrible things to their own people in the name of atheism. And they were not led by a handful of extremists; they were led by large numbers of officials who enacted policies for entire nations. Yet somehow this fact escapes the notice of those who want to portray only religious people in a negative light.

Many young people have read these books and have been deeply influenced by them. These books automatically classify religious ideas as illogical. They portray people who hold to a sincere faith in God as naive or uneducated at best, and at worst, as using faith to deliberately manipulate people's emotions for selfish gain. From my conversations with many young people who are seeking to deconstruct Christianity, I can summarize their train of thought as being something like this:

1. Evil exists in the world.
2. If God is real, He would stop evil things from happening.
3. Since God has not stopped evil, He must not exist, or if He does exist, He is not worthy to be followed.
4. Since intelligent people feel this way, anyone who does not feel this way must not be intelligent.
5. Christians, therefore, must be categorically ignorant and/or illogical.

Obvious variations on that flow of logic exist, but the basic ideas are essentially the same. Antireligious people say this is a logical conclusion based on reasoning and facts, but if we examine the flow of ideas carefully, they are not based on logic but on opinions. These opinions are often based on emotional reactions to the presence of evil. For example, someone might say if there really were a God, He would eliminate suffering in the world. While many may sympathize with that statement, it is an emotional statement, not a logical one.

Pain and suffering will always exist in the world. Removing God from the picture will not remove pain from the world. If anything, removing God from the equation only makes the situation worse. The people who hold to these views feel a certain way about God and a certain way about people who believe in God. They think their feelings are right and everyone else's feelings are wrong. Though they may sincerely believe their arguments are based on logic, those arguments are more often based on feelings and are no more logical than the arguments Christians may give for how they feel God in their lives.

Postmodern people need Christians to help them think through a more logical path to discover truth. However, since postmodern people are not going to accept everything carte blanche, they need time to process information and evaluate that information through the filter of their own experiences and relationships.

It can be an exasperating process for Christians to share their faith with skeptics from the younger generation. While older generations may have had a general knowledge of the Bible and perhaps some general acceptance of it as a historical book, younger generations have very little biblical background. Often what they do know is gleaned from books, YouTube videos, or blogs that attack the Bible, making their understanding of it skewed in a negative way.

As exasperating as it may be, sharing our faith with our young friends is important because the Bible reminds us in Romans 10:17, "Faith comes from what is heard, and what is heard comes through the message about Christ" (HCSB). The gospel has great power to supernaturally break through the emotional arguments young skeptics make. It is vital for Christians to re-engage young skeptics in honest discussion.

While some young skeptics are genuinely searching for truth, others are just looking for someone to argue with. I often encounter individuals my friend Adrian Despres refers to as "dishonest skeptics." He travels across the nation speaking to young adults about issues of faith. He has debated a number of self-proclaimed anti-God experts, including Dr. Terry Cousins from the University of South Carolina, a geology professor in Memphis, and a group of atheists in a series of televised debates in Traverse City, Michigan.

> **While some young skeptics are genuinely searching for truth, others are just looking for someone to argue with.**

Despres says that dishonest skeptics are people who claim to be looking for truth but actually have already made up their minds about what they believe. They are not really interested in learning the truth; they simply want to argue with anyone who will listen. Perhaps they like the attention, or perhaps they think they will win people to their cause through their aggressive actions. Despres calls them dishonest skeptics because they have lied to themselves about being open minded. Dishonest skeptics are narrow minded and have closed themselves to learning and growing. Dishonest skeptics frequently accuse Christians of ignoring the facts, yet when Christians show them the facts, dishonest skeptics choose to ignore them.

One reason it can be frustrating to talk to dishonest skeptics is that they tend to change the rules mid-conversation. For example, they may say they cannot accept the Bible as truth for a certain reason, but when they are shown a logical way to resolve that particular conflict, instead of accepting the logical reason, they discard the logic and simply come up with another reason for not accepting the Bible. And if they are shown the answer to that objection, they just come up with yet another reason. The reality is that they have already decided they are not going to accept the Bible as truth, and no amount of logical discussion will convince them.

In early 2008 I met Thomas Youngfellow,[2] who had grown up in a home that was very strict in its religious views but lacked emotional depth or warmth. His parents often kicked him out of the house for minor issues, while espousing belief in God at the same time. Thomas's parents bounced from church to church, always finding fault with the pastor or other leaders in the church.

It was not surprising when Thomas rebelled against his parents' unhealthy religious expression and experienced what he calls a "de-conversion." Though Thomas enrolled in college for a time, he did not complete his bachelor's degree. He eventually moved back in with his parents because he was unable to find a job that could fully support him. He spends much of his time surfing the Internet for articles about how religion is evil and God is immoral. In one conversation with Thomas, I pointed out how he was simply replacing God's opinions for his own opinions. He responded by saying if he had to choose his opinions or God's opinions, he would go with his own ideas. He trusts himself more than he trusts God.

That is simply not a logical conclusion for a young man in his situation. After all, he lacks a complete college education. He is underemployed. He is in a constant state of tension with his parents. He has alienated most of the friends. He is often depressed and angry. Despite all this, he thinks his opinion is better than God's, and no amount of logical discussion with him can move him from his position. Though Thomas tells himself he is a seeker of truth, many people who have discussed issues of faith with him have concluded that he is a dishonest skeptic.

I do not consider myself a great philosopher or one of the finer orators of logic, but based on my experiences when dealing with young skeptics, I suggest that they might want to consider this path of logic toward God:

1. The incredible level of organization in the universe is mathematically improbable without an intelligent designer behind it.
2. The sheer number of supernatural events that happen in the world indicates that designer is a supernatural being, which many cultures would call God.
3. If such a supernatural designer (God) exists, that God must have designed the universe for a purpose.
4. If we discover that purpose, our lives will have more meaning because we will then understand why we are experiencing life to begin with.
5. Since only God knows our purpose, if we come to know and understand God, we are more likely to discover our purpose.
6. Therefore, we must make knowing and understanding God a key priority in our lives.

This logical path toward God does require a certain level of faith, but it is not a blind leap of faith. It is a more-logical path toward faith. Each logical fact that is established is a step toward a rational belief in God. Each step of faith is based on facts that have already been established. Therefore, it is not illogical to take a step of faith if the previous steps were based on facts. A number of points exist to support this flow of logic.

Step one in a logical path toward faith begins with the understanding that the incredible level of organization in the universe is mathematically improbable without an intelligent designer behind it. Scientists are amazed at the complex level of order in the universe. Whole websites have been dedicated to this reality, such as http://designanduniverse.com, which gives an array of articles about how the design of the human body, the level of order in plant life, and the complex level of design in the animal world show the fingerprints of a designer.

It is not just theologians who see these designs in nature. John Ashton, an Australian research scientist with a PhD from the University of Newcastle, where his dissertation won the university's educational research prize, recently edited *In Six Days: Why Fifty Scientists Choose to Believe in Creation.*[3] As the title suggests, it contains articles written by fifty different scientists who see God through science. *Mere Creation: Science, Faith & Intelligent Design,*[4] edited by William Dembski, an analytic philosopher and a senior fellow at the Discovery Institute's Center for Science and Culture, contains articles from nineteen experts who are trained in mathematics, mechanical engineering, philosophy, astrophysics, ecology, and evolutionary biology. Each article debunks materialistic naturalism on both scientific and philosophical grounds. Additional books by scientists espousing some form of intelligent design in the universe are being published regularly as increasingly more and more scientists see evidence for a designer in nature.

The field of mathematics also supports the concept of a designer. Mathematicians have calculated that "the mathematical probability of a single cell coming about by chance is 1/10340,000,000."[5] For those who struggle with fractions that big, it means that it is a fraction of one divided by one followed by 340 million zeros. Even if a single-celled organism did somehow arise from nothing, for it to develop into a complex life form would have required countless numbers of mutations. Any eighth-grade science textbook will tell you that most mutations are negative, not positive. This makes it extremely improbable that a single cell mutated into something more complex. These mathematical facts create extreme difficulties for the concept that life arose on its own without an outside force directing it. These are just a few of the logical arguments many highly educated people have agreed lead to the logical conclusion that there is a higher power at work in the universe. But those who refuse to see God in any of these logical arguments ignore rational thinking in their efforts to remove God from their worldview.

Step two in a logical path toward faith includes an understanding that the sheer number of supernatural events that happen in the world point to the designer being a supernatural being. Jeffrey Long, a physician practicing radiation oncology in Tacoma, Washington, sits on the board of the Near Death Experience Research Foundation. That group has collected over twenty-five hundred extensive accounts of people who have had various supernatural near-death experiences. These people come from all walks of life, various religious backgrounds, and many different nations. Dr. Long concludes, "Medical evidence fails to explain these reports and … there is only one plausible explanation—that people have survived death and traveled to another dimension."[6] So many people have had near-death experiences with such remarkable similarities that it is logical to conclude that something exists on the other side of death.

Supernatural experiences do not just exist on the other side of death. Miraculous events also happen in our lives all the time. According to a Pew Research Center study published in February 2010, "Nearly 80 percent of all Americans, in fact, say they believe in miracles."[7] This staggering belief in the miraculous cannot just be coincidence or imagination. The sheer number of people who testify to having experienced miracles in their own lives leads to the logical conclusion that there must be some supernatural power at work in the universe.

We know this supernatural being is still involved in the lives of individuals because this being listens to and responds to prayer on a regular basis. Numerous scientific studies on prayer show that prayer actually works.[8] Because prayer can be a very subjective experience, double-blind tests were used. In double-blind tests neither the people being tested, nor the administrators controlling the tests, knew who was being prayed for until the test results were tabulated. This ensures that no one's personal bias for or against prayer can impact the outcome of the experiment. In these double-blind tests, people who were prayed for healed faster than those who were not prayed for. Studies conducted in a number of different settings showed the same results: the people who were prayed for healed faster. In any other field, such a staggering amount of evidence would be adequate proof, but people who hold to an anti-God worldview refuse to accept the evidence. Those who really want to be logical, though, must conclude that the supernatural exists.

Once these two first steps in a logical path to God are laid down using scientific evidence, the rest of the steps begin to fall into place. If the universe has a Creator, that Creator must have made the universe for a purpose. Each part in that creation, including mankind, must be a part of that purpose. If people can discover what their part in the purpose is, they can fulfill that purpose more completely. Though there might be many ways of discovering that purpose, the most direct way is to learn and understand the Creator who initiated the purpose. Therefore, the most logical course of action is to search for a relationship with and understanding of the Creator and make it a key priority in life. Though some faith is required to accept that the Creator is God instead of space aliens or some other intelligence, it is not blind faith; it is informed faith based on logical presuppositions.

We could debate various points of logic without end. But at some point, we have gathered enough data to move beyond debate and start drawing some logical conclusions. Those conclusions, when based on facts, can give us the confidence we need to know there is a God and that He wants to be involved in our lives. Love compels us to help those who are not yet at the point of drawing such conclusions move to such a point. Below is a modern parable I wrote that I often give to people who are struggling to make that final step of faith.

"Josh's Logical Step of Faith"—a Modern-Day Parable

There was once a little boy named Josh. He was fascinated by science and wanted to know how everything in the universe worked. Even as a little boy, Josh asked complicated questions that had only complicated answers. When Josh grew up, he got a job in a scientific laboratory working for the famous Dr. Reason. Dr. Reason was well known for doing excellent research and producing scholarly reports about that research. As the years passed, Josh was able to be part of exciting research that answered many of his questions about how the universe worked. When Dr. Reason finished a major project, he always published an article in a well-respected scientific journal. The research was meticulous, and the conclusions were rational. Dr.

Reason was so careful in his research that no one had ever proven wrong any of the conclusions in his articles. Josh respected Dr. Reason for the research he did and for the solid conclusions in the articles Dr. Reason published.

The longer Josh worked for Dr. Reason, the more their relationship evolved. In time, they became great friends—perhaps even best friends. Dr. Reason would remember little details about Josh and use those details to make Josh's life more joyful. For example, Dr. Reason remembered that Josh liked chocolate cake, and so he would bring chocolate cake to the lab when it was Josh's birthday. Though Josh did not have quite as good a memory as Dr. Reason, over time he realized that Dr. Reason like baked chicken. Because of this, Josh would often bring baked chicken to the lab for lunch and share it with Dr. Reason.

Dr. Reason was also willing to help Josh when he needed it. When Josh's car broke down, Dr. Reason gave him a bonus in his paycheck. When Josh's grandmother passed away, Dr. Reason came to the funeral and sat next to Josh. Though Dr. Reason's scientific research and scholarly articles meant a lot to Josh, it was all these other things that really made Josh and Dr. Reason friends.

One day Dr. Reason published an article in a journal about a project he had been working on in a different laboratory. Josh knew that Dr. Reason had a number of other labs where he was also doing research. Josh was vaguely aware of what was going on in those labs but did not know all the details like he did in his own lab. When the new article came out, many people did not like Dr. Reason's conclusions. Josh did his best to defend Dr. Reason's work, but since he did not know all the details of what was being done in those other labs, he was not able to give as good an answer as he might have liked. Josh asked Dr. Reason for details, but the research was so complex that Josh really could not fully understand the explanation. Josh tried to explain to others what he did understand, but his explanations were inadequate.

People began to pressure Josh to abandon his friendship with Dr. Reason. People said Josh's faith in Dr. Reason had blinded Josh to the truth, but Josh was not moved from his belief in Dr. Reason's abilities or intelligence. Josh patiently explained to others that while he was indeed exercising faith in Dr. Reason, it was not blind faith. From Josh's perspective, it was only a small step of faith, not a giant leap of faith. Josh's faith was based on his past experiences with Dr. Reason. Josh had this perspective because Josh knew Dr. Reason really well. Dr. Reason had proved himself to Josh, not only in the scholarly research and well-written articles but also in their friendship. It was not blind faith but informed faith that Josh placed in Dr. Reason.

Many people could not understand Josh's perspective. At first Josh was frustrated with these people, even a little angry at some of them. In his frustration, Josh said a few things he should not have. But in time Josh realized these people could not understand because they did not know Dr. Reason the way he did. Though Josh really did want to know all the details about Dr. Reason's other project, he knew Dr. Reason well enough to accept that in time, all would be revealed. Josh was comfortable in his logical step of faith and remained Dr. Reason's lab assistant. Many people did not understand Josh's choice, but Josh knew it was the right one, so he was at peace with his choice even if others did not understand it.

What is the meaning of this parable? Many people say that Christians blindly follow a God for which there is no scientific proof. But to Christians, God is revealed both in the Bible and in their personal experiences with Him. Christians read the Bible and find parts of it very easy to understand and explain to others. Other parts of the Bible are more difficult to understand and explain. Christians have built such a close relationship with God that they have faith to believe in the more difficult aspects of His will and ways. Those who are not Christians may call it blind faith or a leap of faith, but for Christians who have a personal relationship with God, it is not a blind leap of faith at all. It is more a logical step of informed faith than a blind leap. Though others may lack the ability to understand that informed step of faith, to Christians it is simply the next step on the logical journey toward a God of truth.

Using logic as an evangelism tool can be delicate work because words can be twisted out of context and made to prove points that clearly are not accurate. However, if we hope to reach young people with the gospel, we must learn to use some level of logic in our efforts.

Many honest skeptics are sincerely looking for truth. We should seek to answer their questions not only with Scripture but also with logical conclusions based on evidence God has clearly built into the universe He designed. We can also expect to encounter dishonest skeptics who just want to argue. Dishonest skeptics are a greater challenge because, despite their claims to be open-minded, they are not actually interested in learning from other perspectives.

Christians must be careful not to their waste precious time and energy arguing and debating with those who are not interested in hearing the truth. Instead, Christians should focus on those who are actually looking for truth. Christians should help honest seekers discover the logical path toward God. Though that path will require faith, it does not require blind faith. Christians must remember John 6:44, which teaches, "No one can come to Me unless the Father who sent Me draws him" (HCSB). When the Spirit begins to draw people to Christ, those people begin to see God in various ways because God will reveal Himself along the way. A realization of God's presence stirs up faith in them, which allows them to look more earnestly for God. The result is that when they finally come to faith, it seems like the most logical conclusion they could possibly make.

Christians who want to witness effectively to young people will trust more in the Spirit and less in their own debating skills. That does not mean Christians should not be able to defend the faith. It simply means that once we have shown people the truth, we must step back and give those people time to process what we have shown them and give the Spirit time to work in their lives. Arguing from anger never produces positive results. While we wait for young adults to process what we have shared with them, we must engage in earnest prayer for them. James 5:16 reminds us, "The prayer of a righteous person is powerful and effective" (NIV). We should never underestimate the power of prayer. In our evangelism efforts, it is a tool that that can soften the hardest heart.

CHAPTER ELEVEN

WHAT TO DO WHEN THE NEXT GENERATION FINALLY COMES TO CHURCH

With a vision to obey the Great Commission, churches must become intentional in their efforts to reach the next generation. Churches who seek to reach out in evangelism will venture outside the walls of their buildings and into the communities around them. Churches will engage the culture with the gospel by meeting specific community needs, helping the less fortunate, viewing evangelism as more of a process than an event, helping young people deal with pain, and explaining why it is logical to believe in God.

Only after we use these techniques to build bridges to postmodern people will many of them be interested in discovering who Christ is in their personal lives and attending church. We want them to have a positive experience when they finally decide to visit a church so they will continue to progress in their spiritual journey. We want them to continue to learn and process what it means to be part of the body of Christ through meaningful involvement in a community of faith. Yet we cannot give up biblical principles to please postmodernists. Otherwise we will have defeated the purpose of all our efforts to share such principles with them in the first place. Therefore, we will want to ask ourselves what we will do to help young people have a worship experience that is both culturally relevant and biblically sound when they finally come to church.

Based on my experience with young people, there are six things we can do in our worship services that will speak to the culture of young people without violating biblical principles.

1. Use a lot of technology.
2. Maintain a sense of the sacred.
3. Have music that will move them closer to God.
4. Have a worship service that is experiential.
5. Use sermons that are delivered passionately and include relevant application to real-life issues.
6. Help all who visit feel like they belong.

Postmodern people live in a very technological world. They have come to expect technology to play a significant role in their lives. Because postmodern people grew up surrounded by technology, it is the only way many of them know how to learn. Churches can use this to their advantage by becoming good at utilizing such tools. If we as leaders do not know how to use technology, we may want to invest some time in learning how. There is nothing unbiblical about projecting the words of the songs or the notes from the sermon on the wall. It does take time to prepare, and it does take some advance planning. It does impact the level of organization that is required to put a worship service together. However, churches that are reaching the next generation are investing time and effort into such advance planning.

It might be worthwhile to consider what the Bible says in 1 Corinthians 14:40, "But everything must be done decently and in order" (HCSB). Using technology in the worship service is simply taking that planning and organization to another level. Technology can also be used before or after the worship service to encourage discussion and Bible study. Facebook is a great tool for posting review questions or to initiate follow-up discussions based on the sermon. Many churches have small-group ministries. For many young people, Facebook groups are one expression of the small group of the future.

When we invest time and resources to learn how to use technology effectively in worship services and ongoing ministries, we will reap rich rewards.

Though technology is important to the next generation, churches must balance the use of technology with a sense of the sacred. While the majority of young people may have wandered from the church traditions of their childhood and may even question the historical teachings of the church, they often still have a vague memory of the sacred. Since many people in these situations grew up in more formal worship environments, they often believe some of the more formal elements of worship are sacred. Therefore, churches seeking to reach postmodernists should rediscover some of the more liturgical aspects of worship, even if that is not typical of their particular worship style.

For example, many postmodern people have enough past connection with church to grasp that the Lord's Prayer is meaningful. Therefore, they expect to recite it when they come to church. Likewise, they may think that candles are appropriate for a worship setting. Therefore, churches may want to add some candles to their sanctuary if they do not already use them. Postmodernists understand that taking communion is something special, even though they may not have participated in it in some time. Churches need to help them relearn what communion is and explain the steps required to be able to receive communion again.

Members of the next generation seldom know the meaning of all these religious rituals, but in their minds, such traditions are all part of the sacred aspects of church. Though some evangelical churches shy away from such formal expressions of faith, we may want to prayerfully consider incorporating more of these elements into our worship experience.

It is important to note that there is no need to adopt all the practices of liturgical churches. After all, people are leaving those churches because they find the services to be dry and dull. However, combining one or two of the more liturgical elements with the use of technology, vibrant music, experiential worship, passionate preaching, and a welcoming atmosphere creates a powerful experience for postmodern people.

Faith Community Church in Barre, Vermont, uses a high degree of technology in its services. All the songs are projected on the wall, as are the Scriptures and notes from the sermon. It is not unusual for a video to be incorporated into the service. Despite the use of technology, Faith Community Church also lights candles before their services, quotes the Lord's Prayer at almost every service, encourages people to use kneeling benches, and celebrates communion together much more frequently than many churches in the Southern Baptist Convention, of which they are a part. Combining these technological and sacred elements has allowed Faith Community Church to connect to a large number of young people. Churches can use technology in innovative ways without losing the sense of the sacred during a worship service.

Churches will also eventually have to discuss the delicate issue of what type of music to use in worship. The language of today's young adults is music. Churches that understand this new language will be able to reach young adults more effectively. Many churches falsely think that if they just add drums or guitars to their worship services, then they will automatically reach young people. While it is true that most young adults prefer music that has more bass and is more upbeat than traditional Sunday-morning fare, just speeding up the tempo and adding a drum will not keep young people coming to church.

The secret to communicating to young adults through music is to understand that young adults use music to express their emotions. For young adults, music is how they communicate with those around them. They sing about their experiences and how those experiences make them feel. They use song lyrics as Facebook posts and in text messages to communicate how they feel about themselves, other people, politics, and their personal experiences, as well as what they think about spiritual issues. Danny Ferguson is a professional youth minister serving with Youth for Christ in Langley, Canada. When discussing the critical issue of music, Ferguson says "Music can be a gateway to understand life and God."[1]

Churches sometimes resist changing their music by accusing more modern Christian music of being shallow. While it is true that in the 1970s much of the praise music seemed like it used five words repeated ten times, which resulted in theologically weak lyrics, praise and worship music has significantly evolved in the past forty years. Modern praise music is no longer shallow. Those who persist in thinking this fail to grasp the depth of adoration for God that wells up from deep within young adults when they sing and play music to the Lord.

While young people do prefer the music to be upbeat, what is more important to them is that the music is filled with spiritual passion. Paul Baloche is a worship leader and prolific songwriter of many top contemporary Christian songs, including, "Open the Eyes of My Heart," "Above All," "Hosanna," "Offering," and "Your Name." Writing about the growing desire for authentic worship among young adults, Baloche says:

> I've found that this generation is not looking for another show, another competition, or another place to feel inadequate. They seek authenticity. They seek people who are genuine through and through. Worship is supposed to be the heart's cry to its maker. The leaders in worship should be focused on a genuine expression of the heart, not simply a performance.[2]

Though many criticisms of the worship music of the past were genuine, the growing desire to actually connect with God in a real way is what is now fueling young adults to worship God intently, even if their style of music is not the typical in many churches.

Skeptics of modern Christian music run the risk of following the example of Michal, the wife of David, who despised David's passion for worshiping the Lord in 2 Samuel 6. In the Bible, music was a personal interaction between worshipers and God. Psalms was the early hymn book of the church. When we read the Psalms, we see intimate personal exchanges between a holy God and His people. That is why many modern worship songs are drawn from the Psalms or other Scripture passages. Though more traditional Christians may not like to admit it, many modern worship songs are far more biblical than some traditional hymns because they are drawn directly from Scripture and sung directly to God, which was the original intent of the Psalms.

Since young people often use music as a means of communication, they prefer music that allows them to talk to God instead of just about God. They want their music to be a conversation with the Living God; they do not just want it to state theological facts about God. That is why young people often do not like singing hymns. They may find some hymns too impersonal because hymns often talk about God in the third person. Young people want to talk to God directly. They do not want to sing, "I will praise Him." They want to sing, "I will praise You."

It is interesting to note that some of the older hymns that are more of a conversation with God are actually coming back into popularity because the next generation has discovered that those hymns express to God exactly what young adults are feeling. For example, "Be Thou My Vision," an old Irish hymn written by Dallan Forgail in the sixth century and translated into English in 1905 by Mary Byrne, has become one of the most beloved songs of the next generation looking for a vision from God. A number of young musicians have taken old hymns

> **Churches willing to select songs that either already speak directly to God, or can be converted into such communication with God, will find young adults more interested.**

and changed the pronouns from the objective third person to first person, thus addressing God directly and expressing their love for the Lord in a fresh way. Churches that are willing to select songs that either already speak directly to God or that can be converted into such communication with God will find young adults are more interested.

Young people's preference for a band instead of just a piano and organ can be a challenge for a congregation that is used to traditional accompaniment. To find solutions to this difficult issue, we must turn to the Bible for guidance. When we read Psalms, we see that a number of instruments were used.[3] Worship was a celebration in the

Bible, yet far too many churches have turned it into a formal program instead of a personal interaction with God.

Regardless of how comfortable we may be with our own sacred music traditions, churches that desire to reach today's young adults will work through this issue and come to terms with the reality that music is a key factor in reaching them. The next generation wants to sing to God, not just about God. They want a variety of musical instruments. They would prefer that at least some of the music be more upbeat, though they enjoy quiet songs as well when they are used in a time of reflection and contemplation. If churches can learn to speak the same musical language as these young adults, they may be surprised at just how many young adults will become committed to the church.

Another hallmark of today's postmodern young adults is that they are experience-oriented. They are not as interested in sitting in a classroom hearing about rock climbing as they are in actually climbing a rock wall. They are not as interested in learning about acting theory as they are in actually standing on the stage and performing. They are not as interested in reading about South America as they are in visiting South America, meeting the people, speaking the language, and eating the food. That today's postmodern young adults prefer to be fully engaged in what they are doing has given rise to extreme sports and other experience-based adventures.

Many churches have struggled to keep young adults attending worship services because they offer little in the way of experiences during typical worship services. While some cutting-edge churches are experimenting with new kinds of worship, perhaps we should consider going back to the ancient ways of the early church. In the early church, a large group did not sit and just listen to a person speak. They often interacted with the speaker and asked questions. Paul even had to address this in one of his letters to the church of Corinth because the question-and-answer time had gotten out of hand and begun to distract from the point of worship (1 Cor. 14:26-40). But Paul did not discourage the discussion-based lessons. Instead he gave directions for how to make them more effective.

Early worship also utilized the experience of communion much more frequently than many evangelical churches today. They actually passed a loaf of bread around the room on a regular basis, and each person broke off a piece and ate it. That is so different from the once-a-quarter prepackaged communion wafers some churches use today. Even baptism was a bigger experience in the early church than it often is today. The early church only practiced full-body immersion of adult believers. Full-body immersion of an adult believer is a much more powerful experience than a few drops of water sprinkled on the head of an infant, which is often how baptism is practiced today.

In the Bible, even the music was experiential. They clapped, they danced, they raised their hands, and they responded to God in worship with their entire bodies. Prayer was experiential in the early church. Jewish men raised their hands in prayer and rocked back and forth as they called out to God. The reality was that in the first century, every aspect of worship was experiential. Somehow we have twisted worship into a program where we are spectators rather than being participants in an experience we have with the Creator of the universe. Young adults sense that program-based worship is lacking something significant even when they are unable to articulate what it is. We must return to biblical worship, which has a strong element of experience, if we hope to reach postmodern people.

Young adults are not only looking for experiential worship, but they are also drawn to passionate preaching that is relevant to daily life. Some churches think they can only attract younger adults by watering down the sermon. We demonstrated in chapter 6 that watering down the gospel message actually produces the opposite result because postmodernists believe there is no point in going to church if nothing the church believes has substance anyway. Other churches have attempted to force the gospel message on those who attend. This has not worked either because young adults do not simply accept what they are told; they want to discover it for themselves. That is why they are drawn to passionate preaching that is relevant to daily life. They do not just want a passionate communicator; they also need that communicator to connect whatever is being said to real-life experiences.

Christ Memorial Church in Williston, Vermont, a small community near Burlington, has become well known for its bold but relevant gospel-centered preaching. The sermons, which often last forty-five minutes or more, speak to relevant issues in the lives of postmodern people but hold firmly to biblical teaching. As a result, Christ Memorial has excelled in recapturing people who grew up in church but dropped out because they just did not see any connection between the sermon and real life. Many people in the congregation previously had a connection with various mainline Protestant churches and sensed that the lukewarm sermons were not helpful in their spiritual development. They typically strayed away from church for many years until they discovered the bold and relevant teaching at Christ Memorial. Christ Memorial is a great example of how a church can use passionate preaching that is also relevant to real-life issues.

Churches like Christ Memorial have discovered the following keys to relevant, passionate preaching. Their leadership bases the sermon on a key passage of Scripture. Postmodern people expect something in a sermon other than the pastor's opinion or some pop psychology thinly disguised as a sermon. Therefore, the entire lesson should be wrapped around a single Scripture passage if at all possible. Using a large number of additional verses that are not part of the main text is often counterproductive because most postmodern people are biblically illiterate. They do not know all the Bible stories or where the books of the Bible can be found. Jumping around from passage to passage is very confusing to them.

Since most young adults do not know the stories in the Bible, if we refer to biblical stories as illustrations, we are going to have to take the time to tell that story to the audience. We simply cannot assume they already know it. The same would be true about using various words that may convey significant meaning to a churchgoing audience but that have no meaning whatsoever to a non-churched listener. If we want to use words such as grace, trinity, mercy, redemption, or born again, they will have to be defined. Otherwise a postmodern audience will have no idea what we are talking about.

In addition to using Scripture effectively, be prepared to discuss deep and complex issues with relevant application. If young adults have made the effort to come church, they want to wrestle with the tough questions about life and discover deep answers to life's perplexing problems. They want to know why evil exists and why there is suffering in the world. They want to know why God lets bad things happen to good people if God really is so powerful. Based on extensive research, Lifeway Christian Resources has discovered that "young adults are allowing these questions to change the way they shop, educate themselves, read, and even listen to music."[4] Lifeway concludes, "It's a mystery to many young adults, both inside and outside of church life, why more Christians don't take their responsibilities [about such issues] more seriously."[5] Effective pastors, teachers, and Christian leaders spend time studying the deep issues and are prepared to incorporate them into their sermons because the next generation wrestles with these issues on a regular basis.

As the sermon draws to a close, it is important to challenge postmodernists to consider how the truth of the Scriptures just taught can be applied to their daily lives. However, it is unlikely that postmodernists will make a commitment instantly. Instead, they should be challenged to think deeply for a period of time and then act on their reflective conclusion at some later point. This is in no way a suggestion that we should no longer give invitations or offer people an opportunity to trust Christ; it is simply a realization that the next generation is going to need more time than may be allotted in a typical closing song of a church service. Inviting them to a prayer room to talk with someone further about the implications of the sermon or giving them an email address or phone number they can text with questions about the sermon may be more effective.

Young adults need to be challenged to reflectively contemplate biblical truth and make a commitment to that truth, but only after they have come to a well-considered conclusion. In my own ministry, I often tell students in advance of certain dates when we will be having a baptism or some other spiritual milestone and ask them to come see me before that date if they are ready to make some type of spiritual commitment. That allows them time to consider making a spiritual decision but does not force them to decide without having thought it through completely. When we get frustrated with how long it takes for young adults to move to a place of commitment, we must remind ourselves of that wonderful biblical truth that says no one comes to the Father unless the Spirit draws him or her. Let us teach and preach the Word, filled with His Spirit, and patiently await the Father to draw the next generation to Himself.

Finally, churches that desire to reach the next generation must work hard at letting all know they are welcome to attend any church services or activities regardless of their religious affiliation or lack thereof. A church must help the members of the community know they are welcome to attend church services and activities even if they are not yet sure if they believe in God. Churches often unintentionally portray their membership requirements as attendance requirements. While churches will obviously limit who may officially join the church to those who agree with the church's doctrine and religious practices, anyone should be welcome to attend a church's worship services. Creating an atmosphere that makes everyone feel welcome in the worship service is important.

CONCLUSION

Churches in small towns and rural areas are finding that their communities are rapidly changing because of an influx of urbanites and progressive ideas that increased use of technology have brought. Those churches are discovering that these changes make it more difficult to reach their communities for Christ. To reach the postmodern people who now live in their communities, many churches are facing critical changes in their thinking and practices. Some of those changes will be relatively easy to implement and will cause little discomfort to current members. Those relatively easy changes can help small churches regain their role as the social and ceremonial centers of their communities. Those changes can also help the next generation view the church building as a place for community events that may not be directly connected to the church but are helpful in building bridges to the unchurched. Many small churches will be able to make these types of adjustments once they take the time to prayerfully consider them.

Other changes will be more significant and will bring a higher level of tension. Churches that choose to engage the culture philosophically will take a huge leap forward to reach the next generation, but it will not be easy. The challenge will be in learning how to engage the culture without adopting the culture. These bigger changes may require an investment of time and energy as the church's members venture outside the walls of the church building to serve the community. They may also push some churches to change their view of evangelism from an event to a process. That change in viewpoint will be a struggle for many.

Churches seeking to help a generation in pain will learn to take risks because it is much easier to recognize deep pain than it is to implement ministries that seek to join God in healing that pain. Churches that desire to help nonbelievers discover the pathway toward God as part of a logical journey undertake a huge task. Church leaders who seek to create a worship experience that speaks to postmodern young adults in ways they can understand, without driving off current church members, will spend significant time in prayer. Such changes will most likely require a release of some traditions, as well as an embrace of modern technology and music, along with a rediscovery of ancient liturgical and experiential worship styles.

None of these are easy steps to take. None should be rushed into. None should be forced on a congregation that is unwilling to make these adjustments. But churches that are willing and ready to reach the world with the gospel will find the next generation is responsive because of their desperate spiritual need.

As this book neared completion, I was discussing its contents with two young adults. Both were raised in Christian homes; in fact, both are the sons of pastors. They are both enrolled in Christian colleges and hope to serve the Lord in their vocations, yet both have struggled to maintain a close walk with God, primarily because finding a church that speaks to their needs as young adults has been difficult.

As we discussed the ideas in this book, both grew excited and kept saying how much they wished the churches they were part of in their college communities would put these types of ideas into practice. At one point, one of the young men pulled out his cell phone and said, "If I record everything you are saying, we can use the recording to teach these ideas to other people." The other young man agreed and began to tell me about software that would convert my words into other types of electronic files—software I did not even know existed.

Without realizing it, they were demonstrating many of the ideas in this book. They were convinced the ideas in this book were true because the ideas matched their own experiences and they have a close personal connection with me, the author. While I only thought about writing a book, they immediately considered how to use technology to spread the word. They assumed they would be personally involved as leaders in spreading the ideas. These two young men have chosen not to abandon the church. They have chosen to remain engaged and teach the churches they are connected to how to reach their peers. It is young people like this who give me great hope for the future of the church.

Endnotes

Chapter One

[1] Noteworthy books that explain how cities are changing:
   1. *Welcome to the Urban Revolution: How Cities are Changing the World* by Jeb Brugmann
   2. *The Global Cities Reader*, edited by Neil Brenner and Roger Keil
   3. *Triumph of the City: How Our Greatest Invention Makes Us Richer, Smarter, Greener, Healthier, and Happier* by Edward L. Glaeser

[2] Noteworthy books and articles that demonstrate how churches are reaching urban areas:
   1. 2 Keys for Reaching a City for Christ by EvangelismCoach.org, www.evangelismcoach.org/2009/2-keys-to-city-reaching/
   2. What We Can Learn from City Reaching Churches by Eugene Hor, http://www.thereformission.net/eugesblog/?p=300
   3. *11 Innovations in the Local Church: How Today's Leaders Can Learn, Discern and Move into the Future* by Elmer Towns, Ed Stetzer, Warren Bird
   4. *Comeback Churches: How 300 Churches Turned Around and Yours Can, Too* by Ed Stetzer and Mike Dodson

[3] Creps, Earl. "Disciplemaking in a Postmodern World." http://enrichmentjournal.ag.org/200204/200204_052_discipling.cfm, (accessed January 29, 2011).

[4] Scarbrough, Elinor and Jan W. Van Deth, editors. *The Impact of Values: Belief in Government*. Volume Four. Oxford University Press: Oxford, New York, 1995, 320.

5   Name changed to protect Li-Jin's privacy.
6   Noteworthy books on postmodern evangelism and church growth:
    1. *Everything Must Change: Jesus, Global Crisis, and a Revolution of Hope* by Brian McLaren
    2. *A New Kind of Christianity: Ten Questions That Are Transforming the Faith* by Brian McLaren
    3. *Love Wins* by Rob Bell
7   "Research Reveals Value of Event Evangelism." http://biblicalrecorder. org/post/2010/07/12/Research-reveals-value-of-event-evangelism.aspx, (accessed July 18, 2010).

Chapter Two

1   "America Becoming Less Christian, Survey Finds." http://www. cnn.com/2009/LIVING/wayoflife/03/09/us.religion.less.christian/, (accessed June 15, 2010).
2   Ibid.
3   Meacham, Jon. "The End of Christian America." http://www.newsweek. com/2009/04/03/the-end-of-christian-america.html, (accessed June 15, 2010).
4   Kwon, Lillian. "Survey: Churches Losing Youths Long Before College." http://www.christianpost.com/article/20090629/survey-churches-losing-youths-long-before-college/index.html, (accessed July 24, 2010).
5   Ibid.
6   Grossman, Cathy Lynn. "Young Adults Aren't Sticking with Church." http://www.usatoday.com/news/religion/2007-08-06-church-dropouts_N.htm, (accessed September 15, 2010).
7   Banks, Adelle M. "Mississippi Most Religious, Vermont Least," http:// www.usatoday.com/news/religion/2009-01-29-faith-state-survey_N. htm, (accessed December 11, 2009).
8   MacDonald, Jeffery. "Evangelicals March North." http://www.csmonitor. com/USA/2009/0731/p02s01-usgn.html, (accessed June 24, 2010).
9   Stetzer, Ed. "Curing Christians Stats Abuse." http://www. christianitytoday.com/ct/2010/january/21.34.html?start=3, (accessed July 10, 2010).
10 Ibid.
11 Ibid.

Chapter Three

1   Hjalmarson, Len. "Kingdom Leadership in the Postmodern Era," http://nextreformation.com/wp-admin/resources/Leadership.pdf, (accessed August 10, 2010).
2   Ibid.
3   Barrick, Audrey. "Survey: Reasons Why Young Adults Quit Church." http://www.christianpost.com/article/20070808/survey-reasons-why-young-adults-quit-church/index.html, (accessed June 15, 2010).
4   Stetzer, Ed. "They Failed to Embrace Relationships." *Outreach Magazine* Jan/Feb 2011:22-23.
5   Ibid.

Chapter Four

1   Tittley, Mark. "Evangelism and Postmodern Youth." http://www.ymresourcer.com/model/pomo3.htm, (accessed Feb. 25, 2011).
2   Stetzer, Ed. "They Failed to Embrace Relationships." *Outreach Magazine* Jan/Feb 2011:22-23.
3   Oppel, Wayne. "The Mosaic Generation: The Future of Christianity: Who are they and How will they change the future?" *Leadership Advance Online*, Issue VII, page 3, (accessed March 3, 2011). http://www.regent.edu/acad/global/publications/lao/issue_7/pdf/mosaic_generation_oppel.pdf
4   Ibid.
5   Zonio, Henry. "Belonging Before Believing," http://www.elementalcm.com/2009/05/19/belonging-before-believing/, (accessed August 28, 2009).
6   Ibid.

Chapter Five

1   Thistlethwaite, Susan Brooks. "The U. S. is Post-Denominational." *The Washington Post.* http://newsweek.washingtonpost.com/onfaith/panelists/susan_brooks_thistlethwaite/2008/02/the_us_is_postdenominational.html, (accessed March 2, 2011).
2   Ibid.

Chapter Six

1 Kunkle, Brett. "How Many Youth Are Leaving the Church?" http://www.conversantlife.com/theology/how-many-youth-are-leaving-the-church, (accessed August 28, 2009).

2 Name changed to protect Michelle Melecson's privacy.

3 Guin, Jay. "The Future of Progressive Churches of Christ: Shrinking Congregations, Part 1." http://oneinjesus.info/2009/03/the-future-of-the-progressive-churches-of-christ-shrinking-congregations/, (accessed Feb. 19, 2011).

4 Vanderklay, Paul. "Liberal Churches Die, Conservative Churches Lie, Where Individualism Takes Us All." http://paulvanderklay.wordpress.com/2009/07/20/of-individualism-liberal-death-and-conservative-dishonesty/, (accessed on Oct 16, 2010).

5 Guin, Jay. "The Future of Progressive Churches of Christ: Shrinking Congregations, Part 1." http://oneinjesus.info/2009/03/the-future-of-the-progressive-churches-of-christ-shrinking-congregations/, (accessed Oct 16, 2010).

6 Mohler, Albert. "Is the Reformation Over?" http://www.albertmohler.com/2010/02/26/is-the-reformation-over/, (accessed October 16, 2010).

7 Ibid.

8 Vanderklay, Paul. "Liberal Churches Die, Conservative Churches Lie, Where Individualism Takes Us All." http http://paulvanderklay.wordpress.com/2009/07/20/of-individualism-liberal-death-and-conservative-dishonesty/, (accessed on Oct 16, 2010).

9 Ibid.

10 Robinson, Anthony B. "A Tale of Two Churches: Mars Hill VS. University Baptist." http://crosscut.com/2010/08/17/religion/20069/A-tale-of-two-churches:-Mars-Hill-vs.-University-Baptist/?pagejump=1, (accessed Oct 16, 2010).

11 Name changed to protect privacy.

12 Personal interview with Jill Flannel (name changed to protect privacy) on October 17, 2010.

Chapter Eight

1 "About Squire Rushnell." http://www.whengodwinks.com/about/, (accessed February 19, 2011).

Chapter Nine

1   Name changed to protect privacy.

2   Read the entire seventh chapter of Romans.

3   Willyard, Cassandra. "Benchmarks: Bhopal Gas Leak Kills Thousands." *Earth Magazine* http://www.earthmagazine.org/earth/article/191-7d8-c-3, (accessed Nov 14, 2010).

4   Ibid.

5   Ibid.

6   "Spirituality May Help People Live Longer." *WebMD* http://www.webmd.com/balance/features/spirituality-may-help-people-live-longer, (accessed Jan. 13, 2009).

7   Ibid.

8   Roizen, Michael and Mehmet Oz. "Feel the Spirit." *The World* day, Dec. 2010.

9   Ibid.

10 Ibid.

11 Ibid.

12 Sato, Rebecca. "Does Religion Make People Happier? Scientists Search to Explain Why People Believe in a God." *The Daily Galaxy* http://www.dailygalaxy.com/my_weblog/2009/02/does-religion-m.html, (accessed August 10, 2010).

13 Ibid.

14 "Are We Happy Yet?" *Pew Research Center Publications* http://pewresearch.org/pubs/301/are-we-happy-yet, (accessed Aug. 10 2010).

15 "Researchers find brain differences between believers and non-believers." *Psycorg.com* http://www.physorg.com/news155404273.html, (accessed Aug. 10 2010).

16 Newport, Frank, Sangeeta Agrawal, Dan Witters. "Religious Americans Enjoy Higher Wellbeing." *Gallup* http://www.gallup.com/poll/144080/Religious-Americans-Enjoy-Higher-Wellbing.aspx, (accessed 10/28/2010).

17 Ibid.

Chapter Ten

1 Noteworthy books that seek to deconstruct Christianity include:
   1. *God is Not Great: How Religion Poisons Everything* by Christopher Hitchens
   2. *The God Delusion* by Richard Dawkins
   3. *The Blind Watchmaker: Why the Evidence of Evolution Reveals a Universe Without Design* by Richard Dawkins
   4. *The Moral Landscape: How Science Can Determine Human Values* by Sam Harris
   5. *The End of Faith: Religion, Terror and the Future of Reason* by Sam Harris
   6. *Breaking the Spell: Religion as a Natural Phenomenon* by Daniel Dennett

2 Name changed to protect privacy.

3 Ashton, John F., *In Six Days: Why Fifty Scientists Choose to Believe in Creation*, New Holland Books, August 2000.

4 Dembski, William A., *Mere Creation: Science, Faith & Intelligent Design*, IVP Academic, September 28, 1998.

5 "Mathematical Probability Shows Evolution is Ridiculous." *Nodnc.com* http://nodnc.com/modules.php?name=Content&pa=showpage&pid=291, (accessed Dec. 21, 2010).

6 http://www.nderf.org/, (accessed Dec. 21, 2010).

7 Conan, Neal. "Do You Believe in Miracles? Most Americans Do." http://www.npr.org/templates/story/story.php?storyId=124007551, (accessed Dec. 21, 2010).

8 Williams, Debra. "Scientific Research of Prayer: Can the Power of Prayer Be Proven." http://www.plim.org/PrayerDeb.htm, (accessed July 12, 2010).

Chapter Eleven

1 Ferguson, Danny. "What Top Ten Songs of 2010 Communicate Youth Culture," http://proyouthworker.blogspot.com/2011/01/what-top-10-songs-of-2010-communicate.html, (accessed May 19, 2011).

2 Baloche, Paul. "Missing a Beat." http://www.ccli.com/WorshipCorner/Article.aspx?ContentId=49e3dcb4-ee38-427b-995a-c08665f6defe, (accessed May 19, 2011).

3   The book of Psalms was the hymn book of ancient Israel and the early Christian church.

Psalms lists a number of instruments that were to be used for worship:

1. Castanets—two chestnuts attached to the fingers and beat together (Ps. 150:5).
2. Cornet—hollow, curved horn (Ps. 98:6).
3. Cymbals—two concave plates of brass that were clanged together (Ps. 150:5).
4. Drum (also called timbrel or tambour)—wooden hoop with animal skins pulled across the frame (Ps. 68:25).
5. Harp—a wooden device with strings attached that made music when the strings were plucked (Ps. 33:2).
6. Organ—reed instrument made of wood, ivory or bone that was similar to the modern oboe (Ps. 150:4).
7. Psaltery—similar to the harp but was bottle-shaped with strings (Ps. 71:22)
8. Trumpet—made from the horn of ram or goat (Ps. 98:6).
9. Zither—ten-stringed instrument (Ps. 144:9)

This list was adapted from: Willmington, H. L. *Willmington's Book of Bible Lists* (Wheaton: Tyndale House Publishers, Inc., 1989), 213.

4   *Context: Engaging the Young Adults of Your Community*, published by LifeWay Press, 2009, Nashville, TN, 36.

5   Ibid., 37

CPSIA information can be obtained at www.ICGtesting.com
Printed in the USA
BVOW070911220312

285734BV00002B/2/P